Davenport's Colorado Wills And Estate Planning Legal Forms

DAVENPORT'S COLORADO WILLS AND ESTATE PLANNING LEGAL FORMS

WITH 2024-2025 UPDATES

written by attorneys Alex Russell and Robert Maxwell

SEE BOOKS AND LEGAL FORMS AT WWW.DAVENPORTPUBLISHING.COM

COPYRIGHT © 2024 -- ALEX RUSSELL

CREATIVE COMMONS LICENSE. This work is also licensed under a Creative Commons Attribution-NonCommercial-NoDerivatives 4.0 International License.

GOVERNMENT WORKS. No claim is made to copyright or ownership of government materials.

SOME STANDARD FORMS. No copyright or ownership is claimed of "standard" forms or leading forms for the state which are provided in this book, but fair use and privilege to use is claimed. Makers of such forms (often state agency or hospital) have agreed by word, action, and implication the forms may be used and copied if no profit is sought and no substantial changes made to them. Such makers if not lawyer or law firm are barred from profit or advantage through practicing law by making forms then limiting use. Authors believe in a religious duty to help people and do charity.

PUBLICATION DATA
(informal, library may use different data)

Names: Russell, Alex, 1972- author ; Maxwell, Robert, 1960- author

Title: Davenport's Colorado Wills And Estate Planning Legal Forms

Other Titles: Davenport's Wills

Description: Davenport Publishing 2023

Suggested Identifiers: 9798820292019; LCCN 2021909030; ISBN 9798748423373

Subjects: LCSH: Wills--United States;
Wills--United States--Forms;
Estate Planning--United States;
Legal Forms

Classification: LFF KF755 .C55 2022 (or as library chooses)
DDC 346.73 Rus--dc23 (or as library chooses)

9 8 7 6 5 4 3 2 1 0 0 0 0 0 2 3

PERMISSION TO COPY AND USE BOOKS FOR FREE

To help people and groups publisher and authors of the book allow mostly free use by giving all a "Creative Commons Attribution-NonCommercial-NoDerivatives 4.0 International License". Most users face no limit on copying, using, holding in library to loan out, or giving out copies.

Basically, as the image below says, any copying or use is OK if it still shows it is by the authors, is non-commercial (nc) with no price charged, and has no derivatives (nd) so no big changes.

(This work licensed under a Creative Commons Attribution-NonCommercial-NoDerivatives 4.0 International License.)

TO GET COPIES OF BOOKS USE WWW.DAVENPORTPUBLISHING.COM OR AMAZON.COM.

EMAIL ANY QUESTIONS TO DAVENPORTPRESS@GMAIL.COM.

WARNING

THIS PUBLICATION IS NOT A SUBSTITUTE FOR LEGAL ADVICE. Publisher and authors say and warn this publication is not giving any legal, accounting, or other professional services or advice, which if wanted can be obtained by consulting in person an attorney or some other professional. **No attorney-client relationship or any relationship creating a duty or obligation is agreed to or created by the purchase or use of this publication or forms.**

**BOOKS AND FORMS FOR OTHER STATES ARE AVAILABLE.
SEE WWW.DAVENPORTPUBLISHING.COM FOR INFORMATION.**

CHAPTER	TABLE OF CONTENTS	PAGE NUMBER
CHAPTER 1	BOOK BASICS AND LIST OF FORMS	1
CHAPTER 2	TERMS, PROPERTY LAW, AND HELPFUL INFORMATION FORM	4
CHAPTER 3	WILL BASICS	8
CHAPTER 4	WILL GIFTS INCLUDING RESIDUE	10
CHAPTER 5	DEBT, MARRIAGE, AND YOUNG CHILD ISSUES	15
CHAPTER 6	BASIC IDEAS ABOUT HEALTH CARE FORMS	18

WILL RELATED FORMS

CHAPTER 7	FORM 1: WILL (STANDARD)	19
CHAPTER 8	FORM 2: WILL (GUARDIAN)	23
CHAPTER 9	FORM 3: SELF-PROVING AFFIDAVIT	27
CHAPTER 10	FORM 4: TANGIBLE PERSONAL PROPERTY MEMORANDUM	29
CHAPTER 11	FORM 5: HANDWRITTEN WILL	31

HEALTH CARE FORMS

CHAPTER 12	FORM 6: MEDICAL DURABLE POWER OF ATTORNEY	33
CHAPTER 13	FORM 7: LIVING WILL	35
CHAPTER 14	FORM 8: MEDICAL ORDERS FOR SCOPE OF TREATMENT (MOST)	37

GIVING POWER FORMS

CHAPTER 15	FORM 9: STATUTORY FORM POWER OF ATTORNEY	40
CHAPTER 16	FORM 10: POWER OF ATTORNEY BY PARENT OR GUARDIAN	46
CHAPTER 17	FORM 11: DECLARATION OF DISPOSITION OF LAST REMAINS	48
APPENDIX	HOW TO GET FORMS AND SAMPLE FILLED OUT FORMS	51

CHAPTER 1
BOOK BASICS AND LIST OF FORMS

ESTATE PLANNING CONTROLS THINGS IF LATER ABSENT, SICK, OR DEAD

This book helps people in Colorado do legal documents to help control their health care, property, money, children, funeral, and more if later they are absent, sick, or dead. Doing this is called "Estate Planning".

ESTATE PLANNING MOSTLY IS DOING SIMPLE THINGS IN 3 AREAS

Estate Planning is mostly doing simple things in 3 areas: <u>Will Related</u>, <u>Health Care</u>, and <u>Giving Power</u>. This book has 11 ready to use Colorado legal forms (but most people use <u>just a few</u> of these forms).

WILL RELATED FORMS

Form 1. Will (Standard) – a Will (also called a Last Will And Testament) lets a person control things after their death like who gets money and property, who is Executor, and if easier legal options can be used.

Form 2. Will (Guardian) – Will with part added to name a Guardian to care for a minor child under 18 if needed (like if both parents later die) and a Conservator to if needed help manage a child's finances.

Form 3. Self-Proving Affidavit – optional form done with a Will to later help use a Will after a death.

Form 4. Tangible Personal Property Memorandum – lets a person easily anytime add more gifts to occur after death, but it can only cover "tangible personal property" like cars, furniture, jewelry, and clothes.

Form 5. Handwritten Will – this Will can be done more easily by skipping the normal 2 witnesses and but by law must be all handwritten by the person doing the Will.

HEALTH CARE FORMS

Form 6. Medical Durable Power Of Attorney – this very popular form lets a person name someone as Agent to if ever needed help control health care and also if wanted write health care instructions.

Form 7. Living Will – does serious action of saying to not provide medical care if <u>later</u> doctors think an incapacitated person has an irrevocable terminal condition and more medical care likely won't help..

Form 8. Medical Orders for Scope of Treatment (MOST) – does serious action of saying <u>immediately</u> to no longer try care listed in the form like C.P.R., and form is short so it can be read fast like by paramedics.

GIVING POWER FORMS

Form 9. Statutory Form Power of Attorney – lets power over money, property, and more be shared during life with a very trusted person like a spouse, adult child, or best friend so they can help do things.

Form 10. Power Of Attorney By Parent Or Guardian – lets a parent or guardian briefly share power over a child under 18 with a person to let them if needed make health care and other decisions about them.

Form 11. Declaration Of Disposition Of Last Remains – lets instructions be given and if wanted person be named to control funeral, burial, ceremonies, and similar matters.

COLORADO LAW ON ESTATE PLANNING COVERS MOST PEOPLE HERE

This book is only for Colorado since Estate Planning law and legal documents do vary between states. <u>Usually a state's Estate Planning law applies if a person's primary residence is here</u> (often called "domicile"). Many judges say "residence" occurs if a person lives in a place and has no clear plans to leave. Later plans to move don't matter till people move. <u>People can stay under a previous state's Estate Planning laws after they move</u> if people <u>always plan to leave the new state</u>. For example, people who move to a new state for months or more for travel, school, projects, or military often keep legal ties to their old state. <u>People often do health care forms for the state a health facility is in</u>. Most immigrants of any kind can do Estate Planning here.

PERSON HAS POWER TO CONTROL THESE THINGS BUT IT'S OFTEN NOT VITAL

Estate Planning to control health care, property, money, children, funeral, and more if later absent, sick, or dead is usually easy to do. It is easy since legally a person mostly has full power to order what they want. Given this usually judges, doctors, and other people mostly just ask: "<u>Based on what a person wrote what did they likely want done?</u>" It is also easy since usually simple words can be used (like listing some property and putting a few names) and since simple legal documents can be used. But often Estate Planning is not vital and worth spending much effort on since (despite what people may think) it often does not greatly change the costs, taxes, delays, and later work in these areas. Benefits seem especially low for young people since only 4% of people die by age 50, and only 0.2% of children before age 18 have both parents die so need legal help. *See Social Security Tables by Felicitie Bell*; *Parent Mortality Census SIPP Paper #288.* Many people spend more energy and money on <u>getting good life insurance</u> to help people they love.

BOOK IS SHORT, HAS FORMS TO QUICKLY SEE, AND USES EMPHASIS

This book is short and may read rough but can be read fast. Long books often lead to misunderstanding of the basics and skimming. This book has legal forms people can quickly see. For emphasis paragraph titles, underlining, and boxes are used. This book capitalizes some legal words like Will, Testator, and Agent but this is optional. To save space some small words are skipped and end quote marks put before punctuation.

THIS BOOK COVERS MAJOR LEGAL IDEAS AND SHOULD SUIT MOST PEOPLE

This book covers the big U.S. legal ideas on Estate Planning and major ways Colorado law is a bit different. This book can't cover all legal issues but should suit most people without some strange situations or wishes. <u>Strange situations or wishes that may need research or a lawyer include</u>: a) strange gift wishes for property and money, b) wealth over $5 million, c) big medical concerns like extreme age, d) property or money going to a person with a disability or special needs, and e) wish to move or hide assets to qualify for government help.

LEGAL FORMS CAN HELP MANY AND THIS BOOK HAS STANDARD FORMS

Legal forms are good at most things involved in Estate Planning and can make binding legal documents. Instead of legal forms a lawyer can be used for Estate Planning but this can be costly, take months of work, and they can make mistakes. In life people often pick a cheaper option. Importantly often a hospital, charity, state agency, or state legislature <u>has made a form most people use and call the "standard form"</u>, and doctors, judges, and other people may not like to follow anything else. This book <u>does</u> provide mostly standard forms.

ANYONE ELSE CAN FILL IN MOST OF A FORM

When filling out a legal form except for signatures the other parts can be filled in by someone not doing a form with good typing or handwriting (pencil is allowed). Once done often people try to keep the original and hand out copies. Some people have everyone sign multiple copies to have many copies with ink signatures.

LEGAL DOCUMENTS MAY NEED TO BE WITNESSED OR NOTARIZED

To be legally valid and enforceable some legal documents need to be "witnessed", which is someone watching the person doing the form sign and then the witness signs too. Some documents need to be "notarized" which means a person who is a "notary" sees it signed and then uses an ink stamp and signs too. Notaries (also called a "notary public") are at some banks, brokers, insurance agents, courts, law offices, libraries, and mailing-copying centers. Using a phonebook to find a notary willing to help is recommended. The words "subscribe" and "execute" means a person signed a document, and "acknowledgment" means a person said a signature was theirs. If a person signs a document in a foreign language it is usually binding. When filling in a form it may help to know "respectively" in a form means "in the order just stated".

SOME LESS COMMON OR LESS USEFUL FORMS ARE NOT IN THIS BOOK

This book skips some possible but less common or less useful documents.

- A "Codicil" can modify a Will but it is easier and legally safer to just rewrite the whole Will.

- Some people do a "Pet Trust" to help a pet, but it's easier to just give money in Will to person given a pet.

- Some people do a "Revocable Living Trust" so a Trust entity with a Trustee holds property or money during their life, usually done to after death have faster transfer of things and avoid small delays, costs, or work of others (by "avoiding probate"). But this is rarely done as it may require moving most of a person's things to a Trust causing maybe years of hassle, mostly to avoid later small work for people happy to be getting things.

- "Childrens Trust" papers can be done (like as part of a Will) so at a death a Trust gets money or property for a minor child to manage until 18, but this is uncommon due to possible cost and hassle, since it rarely matters (as this book explains), and since most Wills already arrange other legal help for young children.

- Though separate forms exist usually organ donation in handled in drivers license or state ID paperwork.

PROBABLY DO NEW FORMS IF DIVORCE, MARRY, HAVE CHILD, OR MOVE

Divorcing, marrying, having a new child, or moving to a new state can have big legal effects, and if any of these events occur it is recommended people do a new Will and other Estate Planning papers soon. To help most states say a Will from another state is still valid if people move but this is not always certain.

USUALLY NO FEDERAL, COLORADO, OR OTHER TAX IS OWED AT A DEATH

Usually no federal tax is owed at a death, including no estate, inheritance, or death taxes, because the "Federal Estate And Gift Tax" only starts when a tax credit is used up that covers $13.99 million of money and property in 2025 and later. Due to changes in law Colorado and its local jurisdictions no longer have an estate, inheritance, or other tax that might be owed at a death. About a third of states have an estate or inheritance tax for certain property there owned by people outside the state, but these taxes usually only apply if there is over $5 million in value there.

CHAPTER 2
TERMS, PROPERTY LAW, AND HELPFUL INFORMATION FORM

THERE ARE BASIC TERMS AND IDEAS IN ESTATE PLANNING

Some legal terms and ideas are basic to Estate Planning.

■ "Estate Planning" is about people doing legal documents to control things if later absent, sick, or dead. After a document is done people are mostly free to sell or transfer property, instruct doctors, or change forms.

■ A "person doing a legal document" and "doing a form" means the form is for and affects that person.

■ A "Will" or "will" (this book uses upper case "W") is a legal document done to control issues after death. The phrase "Last Will And Testament" is used since a "Testament" long ago was a small document done along with a Will to do some things.

■ If no valid Will is done a person is "intestate" and then a dead person's property and money is transferred to a spouse, children, and family as intestate law says. <u>Some people a fine with this</u>. This is covered later.

■ A person who died is called the "decedent" or "deceased". A person getting a Will gift is called "recipient", "beneficiary", or "heir" if related (they "inherit"). "Survive" or "surviving" is to be alive after someone died. The term "descendants" or "issue" usually means a person's children and grandchildren.

■ A person named in a Will to handle things after someone's death is called an "Executor", but if a judge has to pick someone they are called an "Administrator". <u>The new term "Personal Representative" covers both these things and this new term is now commonly used in most Wills in Colorado</u>.

■ A person doing a Will is called "Testator" or "Will maker". Before about 1995 a woman Testator was called a "Testatrix" and woman Executor called an "Executrix" but this is no longer often said or written.

■ "Probate" is a legal process to do things after someone's death like transfer property, handle creditors, and authorize a Guardian. Due to nice changes in law probate is now often informal, faster, and less costly.

■ "Property" is either: 1) "real property" which is land and buildings ("real estate"), 2) "personal property" which is things not real property, like cash, accounts, stocks, tools, clothes, cars, jewelry, and art, or 3) "fixtures" which are things tied to real property (like fences, posts, lighting, and wired-in appliances).

■ A person under 18 is usually called a "minor" and often a parent or guardian helps them do things. A minor or other person not reasonably able to make wise decisions lacks "capacity" and is "incapacitated".

■ A document giving power to someone is often called a "Power of Attorney" where the "Principal" gives power to someone called the "Agent" or "Attorney-in-Fact" (but they needn't be a real attorney or lawyer).

■ Colorado laws are the Colorado Revised Statutes (revised means updated). Each law is often called a "statute" or "section" shown by a "§" or "s" mark. An example of how to cite a Colorado law is: "Colo. Rev. Stat. § 15-11-103". A form put in statutes for people to find and use if wanted is called a "statutory form".

ESTATE MEANS PROPERTY OF DECEDENT AND ENTITY HOLDING THINGS
The "estate" or "probate estate" means <u>all property and money of a dead person</u> that at death or soon after didn't automatically legally go to new owners. Estate is also the <u>name for a temporary entity run by an Executor to do things after a death</u> (it's like a small corporation, e.g., "Estate of John Alan Smith").

PERSON CAN ONLY GIFT IN WILL WHAT THEY OWN AT DEATH
A person can only gift by Will things they own at death <u>so people should research what they do own</u>. Basically by law a person usually owns all they earn as wages and salary, owns their share of income and profit tied to property they own, and owns or partly owns any things their money buys or improves. And for property with "title" documents (real estate or vehicles) or where there is a "listed owner" (like accounts) the named persons are usually the legal owners unless evidence shows special circumstances. Note, a person during life can sell property, make gifts, or transfer things even if they are named in a Will, so <u>people should consider if they already sold or gave away property they also name in a Will gift</u>.

THINGS OWNED IN SPECIAL WAYS MAY LIMIT GIFTING IN WILL
A person should consider if they own real estate or other property in special ownership ways which may limit gifting by Will. Laws vary in different states but <u>some common special ways of ownership are</u>:

- "joint tenant with right of survivorship" or similar legal options, so then property transfers automatically to the other named owners regardless of a Will, which in some states is often how spouses hold their home;
- papers say a "life estate" exists, so then if life of someone ends the other people in papers get item; and
- "Trust property" occurs if paperwork made a Trust entity and then property was transferred into it or this is set to occur, so then the Trust papers control where things put in the Trust go after someone's death.

Plain "joint ownership" with many people owning a thing can occur if people do joint papers, all agree to it, buy with joint funds, or if a gift was to many. Wills <u>can</u> gift joint property, like "I give my half of boat to Ed Hu".

NON-PROBATE TRANSFERS THAT HAPPEN AUTOMATICALLY IGNORE A WILL
It is vital to be aware <u>some money or property of a decedent may automatically transfer on death</u> or soon after to new owners <u>if certain arrangements were made earlier</u>. This is usually called "non-probate property". Such things transfer as arranged even if a Will names the same items in Will gifts.

Examples are: a) a "designated beneficiary" form was done to name people to get an account or investment, b) transfer-on-death accounts were used, and c) real property is held by 2 people as "joint tenants with survivorship" or similar so at a death the surviving person gets things. Usually property in a Trust will ignore a Will and transfers as papers say to. Life insurance usually goes to the named beneficiary.

Trying to do non-probate transfers for all things is called "avoiding probate", but few people try this since it can cause years of hassle, benefits are small, and often some thing is missed. <u>When doing a Will people should consider non-probate transfers that will occur automatically on death and consider what will be left</u>.

HELPFUL INFORMATION FORM CAN HELP TELL FAMILY AND FRIENDS THINGS
<u>People can do an unofficial "Helpful Information" form</u> banks, lawyers, and planners suggest so family or friends after a death will know things. People can staple records or lists to this. <u>See form on next pages</u>.

ESTATE PLANNING HELPFUL INFORMATION

For more space attach copies of form or blank pages. Keep pages by a Will or other place for Executor or family.

1. Personal Information (Name, Birthdate, Social Security number, special family details, other):

2. Real estate, vehicles, and other major tangible property (especially if people may not find them):

3. Non-tangible assets like stocks, accounts, investments, loans owed you, and business interests:

4. Possible income or insurance like pensions, retirement, disability, insurance, or contracts:

5. Debts owed by you like credit card, loan, student loan, mortgage, car loans, and accounts payable:

6. Names and information of professionals used (attorneys, accountants, brokers, doctors, others):

7. Computer passwords and helpful files, document places, and safes or safe-deposit boxes code/key:

8. Other helpful things, wishes for funeral, special requests, and last messages to family and friends:

CHAPTER 3
WILL BASICS

WILL LETS A PERSON CONTROL THINGS AFTER THEIR DEATH

A Will is a legal document done by a person to control some things after their death. A person doing a Will is called the "Testator" or "Will maker". In Colorado a Testator <u>when signing</u> must be at least 18 years old, of sound mind (rational with sufficient memory), and not be under duress (unfair pressure or threat).

KEEP SIGNED WILL IN SAFE PLACE IT CAN BE FOUND AFTER A DEATH

A Will should be kept so it is found within days of a death, like in a desk, drawer, safe, with a person, or less often a safe deposit box. It may help to tell people how to get a Will. Though rarely done Colorado law lets a living person file a Will with a local court for safekeeping. See Colorado Revised Statutes § 15-11-515.

A WILL USUALLY MUST BE SIGNED WITH 2 WITNESSES

WILL MUST SHOW IT'S A WILL AND USUALLY BE SIGNED WITH 2 WITNESSES

In Colorado a document to be a Will <u>must show it is a Will by its words</u>, and the person doing it usually must <u>sign in front of 2 persons</u> acting as witnesses who then sign too. Colorado gives the option to use a notary instead of 2 witnesses but this is rarely done. A notary can be used to do a Self-Proving Affidavit which this book later covers. A Will just spoken on a video or audio recording usually has no legal effect. Note, as this book later explains Colorado law <u>does</u> let witnesses be skipped if a Will is all handwritten.

WITNESSES SHOULD AT LEAST AGE 18 AND OFTEN NOT GETTING WILL GIFTS

A person to witness a Will must be at least age 18. It is best but not legally required a witness not be very old, live far away, or named in a Will to be Executor, Guardian, or similar. In Colorado a Will is <u>still</u> valid if a witness is getting Will gifts and such Will gifts to a witness usually are carried out later. But many people to <u>avoid the appearance of misconduct</u> pick witnesses who are "disinterested" which means they or their spouse are not named to get things in a Will. Often witnesses are friends, neighbors, strangers, and family.

TESTATOR AND 2 WITNESSES SIGN THE WILL WHEN TOGETHER IN 1 ROOM

A person doing a Will usually signs it with at least 2 witnesses who also sign while all are in 1 room and see others sign. People showing others an ID is not required but is common. A Testator need not initial the Will pages. A Testator or witness should <u>use their full legal name</u> unless they greatly dislike and rarely use it. Witnesses only read the 1 paragraph they sign. Most Wills have each witness print their name and address. Legally a Testator needn't say anything but often they say a thing like, "My name is ____ this is my Will that I do voluntarily and ask you 2 people to witness". Lawyers call a person saying a document is their Will as "publishing a Will". Some Testators chat about a Will with witnesses to help show they are of sound mind.

CANCELING OLD WILLS IS USUALLY NOT A PROBLEM

So a new Will is followed old Wills should be canceled ("revoked") but this is easy and rarely a problem. A new Will usually quickly says old Wills are revoked to cancel them, and all this book's Will forms say this. Or people can revoke an old Will by writing "void" or "cancelled" or "X" on it, preferably with a witness to this. Usually crossing out just part of a Will has no effect. Revoking a Will usually doesn't bring back an earlier Will.

OFTEN AT START OF A WILL A PERSON NAMES ANY SPOUSE AND CHILDREN

Many Wills start with a place for a Testator to name any current living spouse and children of any age. Natural or adopted child should be put here including any born outside marriage. People without this family can skip this or put "none". Not doing this may invalidate a Will by indicating a person lacks sufficient mental ability or memory, or let a spouse or child not listed ask a judge to give them a share or all of the estate by saying a Testator just forgot them. After listing family in a Will a Testator is often free to give them nothing.

MOST WILLS SAY TO SKIP COSTLY BOND FOR EXECUTOR AND OTHERS

Most Wills helpfully say no "bond" or "surety" is required for any Executor, Guardian, or similar person. A bond is insurance from a company to insure against misconduct. A Testator usually doesn't want a bond since the persons Testator names are trusted and them later needing a bond will cost the estate money.

A WILL NAMES AN EXECUTOR TO DO THINGS AFTER DEATH

WILL NAMES SOMEONE TO BE EXECUTOR TO DO THINGS AFTER A DEATH

Usually a Will names someone as "Executor" to act after a death like handle debts, find and collect and give new owners property and money, and do probate. The law gives Executors many helpful legal powers. If a Will fails to name an Executor a judge can pick someone, but family may argue about who to suggest. Note, the term "Personal Representative" and not Executor is now often used in Colorado for the person doing things after a death, but these terms mostly mean the same thing. Will gifts can go to an Executor.

EXECUTOR CAN BE PAID AND ESTATE PAYS FOR EXECUTOR'S EXPENSES

Colorado law says normally the Executor can ask to can be paid a fair wage for the time they spend working on an estate. Pay for an Executor may helpfully let money get to this person even if a decedent left little of value and large creditors are asking to be paid. But some Testators don't want such pay and add a Will line about this. In reality most Executors later skip asking for pay so as to not owe income tax and leave more money to carry out Will gifts. Note, expenses an Executor has like insurance, repairs, utilities, funeral, mortgage payments, attorneys, and probate costs or fees are paid for with money or property of the estate. Any lawyer an Executor hires usually is paid hourly or a fixed sum that the lawyer and Executor agree on.

EXECUTOR IS PERSON AT LEAST 21 AND SECOND PERSON RARELY NEEDED

A person to be Executor must be age 21 or older and usually not have a bad criminal record like a felony. A person not residing in Colorado can be Executor but they may need to name a local person to get mail. Naming 2 people to both be Executor is allowed but rare due to the risk of arguments and delays, and since any 1 person named should be trusted. People can name a 2nd person to be Executor if the 1st person is not later available but most skip this since this rarely occurs and if needed a judge can pick someone. To add such a 2nd person a person could add: "or if they're reasonably unable to serve I name ___ to serve".

CHAPTER 4
WILL GIFTS INCLUDING RESIDUE CLAUSE

MAIN USE OF A WILL IS TO SAY GIFTS TO HAPPEN AFTER DEATH

Most people use a Will mainly to say what happens to their property and money after their death, usually by writing down various Will gifts to occur when they die. Verbal and even writings about this are not usually valid if not in a written Will. A Will can control property acquired after it was signed. The very end of this Chapter covers "intestate law" which says where a person's things go at death if no valid Will handles this.

GIFTING IN A WILL USING SIMPLE WORDS OFTEN IS BEST

Making gifts in a Will using simple words is often best, using words like "I give to" and "I gift to". This is legally fine and avoids confusing legal words like "bequest", "devise", and "legacy" which few people know.

A PERSON IS MOSTLY FREE TO GIFT THEIR THINGS AS WANTED

A person is mostly free to give at death their money and property as they want. But creditors a decedent owed money, a spouse, and minor children under age 18 may have some rights which this book later covers.

IN WILL CAN DO SPECIFIC GIFTS TO GIFT PARTICULAR PROPERTY

Most Wills have "specific gifts" to gift <u>particular things</u>. Specific gifts can be any property, like "I give boat to Ed Blom" and "I give UBank account #84553873 to Sue Wu". If a gift is not clear the law assumes all of a kind of thing is given, like "I give jewelry to Ann Po" means <u>all</u> jewelry. But gifting specific property can have surprises like value of items can change, or a Will gift may later fail to occur if property is not owned at death.

IN WILL CAN DO GENERAL GIFTS LIKE OF MONEY

Wills can do "general gifts" where what is gifted is not particular property but can be flexibly chosen, like "I give 1 of my 3 cars to Ed Po" which lets an Executor pick which car. The usual general gift is money, like "I give $5 to Ed Hu". Money gifts are easy to write, let equal gifts be made, and are legally safer for many reasons. To carry out money gifts an Executor usually uses accounts or sells some property in the estate.

RESIDUE CLAUSE IS CATCH-ALL THAT HELPFULLY GIFTS ANYTHING LEFT

Most Wills by their end have a Residue Clause to gift property or money not already gifted in a Will or used other ways, often called a "catch-all" or "left-over" clause. This is covered later in this Chapter.

PERSON IN WILL GIFT USUALLY MUST SURVIVE OR GIFT DOES NOT OCCUR

Many Wills like this book's Will forms say a person named in a Will gift must survive (live past) the Testator for the gift to occur unless gift language specifically says different. If survival is not required for a Will gift what happens if a named recipient is dead can be unclear (state laws can be very complex). <u>People doing a Will should consider how Will gifts to people dying before Testator usually have no effect.</u> People if they see a person in a Will gift has died can re-do a Will or just let the Residue Clause handle it.

CONDITIONS ON WILL GIFTS ARE RARE DUE TO POSSIBLE PROBLEMS

Putting conditions on a gift, like "I give Ann Poe $90 if she graduates college", can cause problems like years of delay, risk of lawsuits, and big attorney's fees. Due to all this conditions are rarely put on Will gifts.

PEOPLE CAN ADD AN ALTERNATE BENEFICIARY LIKE FOR SPECIAL ITEMS

A person named in a Will gift dying before a Testator is rare, and if seen people can re-do a Will to name a new person or let a Will's Residue Clause handle it. Some people to prepare for this chance maybe for special items write an "alternate beneficiary", like "I give boat to Ed Liu but if they don't survive me to Ann Liu".

PROPERTY OR MONEY IN A JOINT GIFT GOES TO MULTIPLE PEOPLE

The same property or money in a "joint gift" can go to many people to each get a part. For example, "I give boat and all hats to Ann Baxter and Mary Ann Swanson" means each person owns part of every item. People later can split things by agreement or an Executor can decide how to divide items. If a person in a joint gift has died their part usually is left to transfer under a Residue Clause.

CAN SAY IF PERSON IN GIFT DIES THEN IT GOES TO LINEAL DESCENDANTS

A Will gift can say it goes to a person but if they don't survive then to their "lineal descendants per stirpes". Descendants are a person's children and grandchildren. "Per stirpes" means "by branch" and is about how to spread property and money, and it mostly tries to divide things so <u>each family branch gets an equal share</u>. Most Wills use "lineal descendants" language in a Residue Clause. <u>An example shows how it works:</u>

A Will may say: **"Clothes to Sue Wu but if they don't survive to their lineal descendants per stirpes"**, and this means if Sue Wu has died and her son Ken Wu is living and her other son Ben Wu has died but left 2 children then, legally, under the law Ken Wu himself gets 50% and Ben Wu's 2 children each get 25%.

GIFT BENEFICIARIES CAN GET PERCENTAGE RATHER THAN EQUAL SHARE

If a Will gift goes to multiple people the law assumes equal shares, but if wanted percentages can be used to make unequal gifts, like "I give boat 90% to John Smith and 10% to Mary Baker".

GIFTS IN WILL CAN GO TO A GROUP OR CLASS OF PEOPLE

To save work a Will gift can go to a group or class of people like certain family <u>if who is meant is later easy to determine</u>. People can say roughly how <u>much in total</u> is gifted to be clearer. Examples are: "I give $10 to each person on my 2018 soccer team" and "I give $10 to each of my grandkids so this is about $100 in total."

AFTER A DEATH FAMILIES OFTEN LET PEOPLE TAKE ITEMS UNOFFICIALLY

Many families <u>unofficially</u> let people take items in ways a dead person said, showed by stickers, or wrote on a note, which is often fine. If anyone objects a judge often has a Will and law be followed fully but later people can voluntarily retransfer items. <u>Later this book covers gifts done by Tangible Personal Property Memorandum.</u>

LATER DIVORCE OR MURDER CANCELS WILL GIFTS

Colorado law says a person divorcing or murdering a Testator usually cancels all Will gifts to the person.

MOST WILLS SAY FAMILY MAY LATER DO INFORMAL PROBATE

Most Wills say after a death the family and friends may do "informal probate" which can avoid costs and delays. Informal probate often is done with just 1 court hearing and often is completed in well under 1 year.

MOST WILLS HAVE A MISCELLANEOUS PART WITH HELPFUL LANGUAGE

Most Wills have a "Miscellaneous" page with paragraphs of legal language to avoid some legal problems. This can help if later legal problems occur. A person doing a Will need not understand these paragraphs.

RESIDUE CLAUSE GIFTING ALL LEFT IS MAIN WAY USED TO GIFT THINGS

THE RESIDUE CLAUSE IS CATCH-ALL THAT HELPS GIFT ANYTHING LEFT

Most Wills by their end have a Residue Clause to gift any property or money not gifted earlier in a Will or used in other ways. Things transferred this way is called the "Residue". Many people gift most their money and property this way by intentionally not mentioning in a Will most things so the Residue Clause handles it. This avoids need to describe things and has less legal risk. After applying a Residue Clause if anything is somehow left then by law a decedent's closest heirs-at-law get things (this is their closest family).

USUAL RESIDUE CLAUSE HAS 2 PARTS

A short 2 part Residue Clause is usual and is used in this book's Will forms, and it has:

1) 1st space to name 1 or more persons to get things if they survive Testator (many name a spouse or closest family here), and if several people are named but only some survive then survivors split things, and

2) 2nd space to name persons to get things if all in the 1st space don't survive (many people name next close family or friends in this space), and if a person in 2nd space has died their descendants get their share.

EXAMPLE OF 2 PART RESIDUE CLAUSE:

"RESIDUE CLAUSE: I give money and property not gifted earlier, the residue:
  a) to ___John Paul Doe my husband___ who survive me with persons just named who survive me taking the share of non-survivors, then if anything remains
  b) to ___Sam Doe, Beth Wu, and Greta Fisher___ and if any of those just named do not survive me their part goes to their lineal descendants per stirpes."

In this example if John Paul Doe has survived he gets all things, but if John Paul Doe hasn't survived and also Sam Doe hasn't survived and he left 2 daughters then those 2 daughters split the 1/3 share of his (so get 1/6 each) and the other 2 persons in the second part Beth Wu and Greta Fisher get 1/3 each.

PEOPLE CAN PUT SAME THING IN PARTS, OR SKIP PART, OR USE PERCENTAGE

Some people put the same 1 person in both parts of a Residue Clause, to fully ensure that 1 person or if they later die their descendants will get things. Or a person with no spouse may skip the Residue Clause 1st part and in the 2nd part put their children (including any who died who had a child), so all branches of a family get an equal share. *See Appendix.* Many people use percentages in the Residue Clause. *See Appendix.*

SOME PEOPLE CHANGE A RESIDUE CLAUSE TO HAVE 1 PART

Some people change a Residue Clause to have just 1 part since this can gift more equally and be easier to understand. *See example in Appendix.* For example a Residue Clause can be made to say:

"The rest, residue, and remainder of my estate, and anything else, I give to _____ who survive me and if any of those just named do not survive me their part goes to their lineal descendants per stirpes."

MUST SUFFICIENTLY DESCRIBE NAMES AND PROPERTY IN A WILL

PUTTING NAMES OF PEOPLE OR GROUPS IN A WILL IS FAIRLY EASY

Putting names in Wills is fairly easy. A judge or Executor assume a person in a Will meant people they know, so common names are OK unless 2 friends or family have the same name. Details can help if names won't be recognized or to be friendly, like "I give $5 to my nurse Sue Ax" and "I give $5 to loyal pal Ed Lee". If people used a nickname "also known as" or "a/k/a" may help, like "I give $5 to Dan Smith a/k/a Old Fishy". Gifts can go to a charity, government, or group, like "I give $10 to The Salvation Army, "I give $8 to Denver Public Library, Colorado", and "I give $5 to Wix Church, Rex, TX". People can phone for a charity's name.

PUTTING DESCRIPTIONS OF ITEMS IN WILL GIFTS IS FAIRLY EASY

Describing items in gifts is easy since people rarely own similar items. Often fine are gifts like: "I give ax to Ed Wu" and "I give big table to Ann Fox". It's OK to gift by category or list, like: "I give tools to Sam Lee" and "I give cow, van, and harp to Sue Hill". Financial assets can use plain words, like "bank accounts" or "stocks", but details can help, like: "US Bank account ending #1511". Gifting using a location is riskier as judges will ignore Will gifts if it seems items were placed to affect gifting and no "independently significant" life reason. So, "I give Ed Po items in safe and desk" judges might not follow, but "I give Ed Po hats in attic" likely is OK.

DESCRIBING REAL PROPERTY IS HARD SO MANY USE RESIDUE OR TITLE

The easier and legally safer way to gift real property (real estate) at death is: 1) do nothing specific so it is handled by a Will Residue Clause, or 2) have a land broker or lawyer put names in a deed or a similar document so the named persons will get the real property at someone else's death.

Gifting real property other ways is harder though possible. Helpfully a Will gift of real property described by location legally does gift all land, buildings, and fixtures located there with no need to describe what's there.

It is possible to gift real property at a particular address with very plain words, like a house, fixtures, and land can be fully given by something like: "I give 81 Maxwell Street, Boulder, Colorado, to Mary Ann Brown".

People can do a blanket gift giving all of a kind of property, like, "I give all real property and fixtures in Adams County, Colorado to Ann Ivy Hill " or "I give all furniture and all bank accounts to Eric Paul Carlson".

Giving real property in a Will using a "legal description" is how many lawyers do it, but this can be hard to do. If using a legal description people must copy without mistakes the full legal description of maybe many lines into a Will with no abbreviation at all. A legal description might be found on a deed or on mortgage papers. Legal descriptions may refer to a "lot" or "blocks" on a map which is recorded in land records of a county, or it may refer to a path around the land borders with various angles, distances, and iron stakes.

CAN LEAVE SOME WILL GIFT LINES BLANK OR WRITE TO SAY SKIP IT

A person writing a Will can choose to not use some gifts lines in a Will legal form, like by just leaving them blank, writing things like "SKIPPED" or "NONE" in them, or using a computer to delete some gift lines. Judges and others usually do not care about neatness or empty spaces in Wills.

MOST STATES AND WILLS SAY PEOPLE TO GET GIFTS MUST SURVIVE 5 DAYS

Helpful laws in most states and all this book's Will forms say if a person dies within 5 days (120 hours) or simultaneously with a Testator, then they are legally seen as dying before Testator. This skips the need to prove exact time of death (like if people die in 1 accident), and avoids a Will gift or right to something going to someone who then soon dies within days (so an item may have to go through multiple probate proceedings).

SIMPLE WILL WITH MOST GIFTING DONE BY RESIDUE CLAUSE IS OFTEN BEST

<u>Writing a simple Will without many gifts, much left blank, and mostly using a Residue Clause is often best</u>.

If there is <u>no spouse and no children</u> often a person does a few small gifts, and then names some family or friends in the Residue Clause to get everything remaining.

If there <u>is only a spouse</u> often a person does small gifts to friends and family, then uses the Residue Clause of the Will to gift all left to the spouse, and then names a few fallback persons in the Residue Clause.

<u>A parent with young children if married to the other parent</u> often does small gifts to friends and family, then in the Residue Clause gives mostly to a spouse, and then names children as fallbacks in the Residue Clause.

<u>A parent with young children if not married or close to the other parent</u> often does small gifts to friends and family, and then uses the Residue Clause to gift all remaining to the children.

INTESTATE LAW HANDLES PROPERTY OR MONEY NOT COVERED BY A WILL

INTESTATE LAW CONTROLS THINGS NOT HANDLED BY A WILL OR SIMILAR

State "intestate" law which is at Colorado Revised Statutes § 15-11-102 to 15-11-103 says <u>if a person dies with no valid Will</u> or <u>if anything is left after Will and transfers are done</u> then some close surviving (living) family get decedent's money and property. Many people like what intestate law says and choose to skip a Will. Note, "descendants" means a person's children and grandchildren, and if someone has died who would get an intestate share often their descendants legally get that share.

Colorado intestate law is a bit complex but it basically says, in order:

First, if there is a surviving spouse and neither the decedent (the person who died) or the spouse have surviving descendants with another parent (like from a previous relationship), then decedent's property and money all or mostly goes to the spouse;

Second, if decedent left a surviving spouse and either the decedent or the spouse have surviving descendants who are not all shared with the other, then the law splits things fairly equally between a spouse and decedent's children with some small modifications;

Third, if decedent left no surviving spouse and no surviving descendants then things usually go to decedent's other nearest relatives starting with decedent's parents, then brothers and sisters, then cousins, and then other close family; and

Fourth, only if none of the above persons survive then decedent's things go to the state of Colorado.

CHAPTER 5
DEBT, MARRIAGE, AND YOUNG CHILD ISSUES

THIS CHAPTER COVERS CERTAIN ISSUES THAT SOME PEOPLE CAN SKIP
This Chapter covers debt, marriage, and young child issues, and some people can skip parts.

DEBT ISSUES

PAYING DECEDENT'S DEBTS MAY USE UP RESOURCES AND REDUCE GIFTS
If a decedent had debts then creditors owed may ask a judge to be paid from decedent's money or property before Will gifts and certain transfers occur. How debts are paid is set by state law and a Will need not describe this. Funds to pay debts comes from decedent's money and property so may affect (in order) the Will Residue, Will general gifts, Will specific gifts, and non-probate transfers. Probate costs, health care, and funeral debts by law have some priority to be paid first. For certain reasons often not all debts are paid. People should consider how paying debts may use up money or property, leaving less to carry out Will gifts. A spouse and family usually aren't liable for decedent's debts unless they actually guaranteed or co-signed.

SECURED DEBTS LIKE MORTGAGE OR VEHICLE LIEN ARE NOT PAID OFF
Laws in most states say do not pay off secured debts on property of a decedent like a house mortgage or vehicle lien even if other debts are paid by Executor or in probate. This avoids using up estate resources on paying these usually big debts and leaves more estate resources to carry out Will gifts and other transfers. Due to this, all this book's Will forms say do not usually pay off any secured debts. But if a Testator wants they can 1) put in a Will an order to pay (like, "Executor pay off the house mortgage"), or 2) gift enough money to pay off a secured debt to the person getting the property. Most banks let the new owners after a death keep paying monthly any secured debt like a mortgage or lien.

FAMILY RIGHTS MAY BE USED TO GET FAMILY THINGS BEFORE DEBTS
Most states have "Family Rights" a decedent's surviving spouse or young children can claim, and this helpfully may let them get things even before most debts of decedent are paid and even before Will gifts.

First, in many states a surviving spouse or if there is no spouse then decedent's children of any age can use an "Exempt Property" right to get some of a decedent's clothing, furniture, tools, and vehicles for family to use to live. In Colorado the Exempt Property right amount was recently $37,000. Colorado Revised Statutes § 15-11-403. Often family can keep even more of decedent's items by claiming decedent gifted them things.

Second, in many states a surviving spouse and young children can use a "Family Allowance" right to get some of a decedent's money and property to live on for 1 year or so. Colorado Revised Statutes § 15-11-404. In Colorado the Family Allowance amount was recently $3,083 if paid monthly or a lump sum $37,000.

Third, in many states a surviving spouse or young children have some right to get (or stay in for years) the house or mobile home owned by a decedent under a "Homestead Law". But Colorado law mostly does not say a spouse or children by law get the homestead property. Colorado law only says if a spouse or children do somehow get the decedent's home then the first $250,000 of equity is safe from creditors (so creditors

can't foreclose unless the decedent owed them quite a lot). In reality often a person has a lawyer or real estate broker put any spouse or children on a house title to get it at the person's death. Note, a normal mortgage on a house usually must be paid each month. No matter what a spouse or children in a home may be legally hard to remove. So family don't try to cause legal trouble about a house usually a person gives a house they own mostly to any spouse or young children. Some people may want to do other research.

MARRIAGE ISSUES

COLORADO USES SEPARATE PROPERTY LAW FOR SPOUSES

Colorado like most states uses the Separate Property Law system that says a married person mostly owns their money and property separately and not jointly with a spouse. Due to this a married person is usually free to sell during life or gift by Will most of their money or property and not have to involve a spouse. But joint ownership by 2 spouses and not separate ownership can arise in other ways, like by agreement, both spouses paying part of the purchase price, if a gift was to both spouses, or if paperwork calls it joint.

COMMUNITY PROPERTY LAW APPLIES IN OTHER STATES FOR SPOUSES

There are 9 states that use the Community Property Law system for spouses (Arizona, California, Louisiana, Idaho, Nevada, New Mexico, Texas, Washington, and Wisconsin). This says property or money is owned 50/50 by spouses as Community Property if it's from mental or physical work while married (like wages or salary) or if items are bought or improved with Community Property. People recently moving from these states may face issues.

JOINT WILL OR SIMILAR WILL BOTH SPOUSES SIGN IS NOT RECOMMENDED

If people worry about future Will change by their spouse they may do a "Joint Will" or "Contract To Make A Will" done by a lawyer saying spouses give all to the other if they die first, then says last living spouse gives to all children equally, and says a spouse may not change this. Most lawyers do not recommend this due to legal issues and some states even ban doing these things. If people are worried about things it is best if they discuss things and maybe get advice of a lawyer.

SPOUSE CAN CLAIM ELECTIVE SHARE INSTEAD OF THEM FOLLOWING WILL

A spouse if unhappy with what a Will and other transfers may give them has a right to instead choose (elect) an "Elective Share" of most of a dead spouse's property and money rather than take what a Will says. Many states do this for fairness, so a spouse has resources to live on, and so early divorce isn't the only way to be financially secure. To avoid this both spouses have to sign a pre-nuptial or a post-nuptial agreement written by a lawyer which can be costly to arrange. Colorado sets the Elective Share at 5% for each year of marriage till reaching 50% at 10 years, and for small estates a spouse maybe can get the first $62,000. Colorado Revised Statutes § 15-11-202. In some cases the Elective Share can cover things decedent gave away or controlled but didn't legally own. Clearly if a spouse uses the Elective Share to get 50% or so of decedent's things this may take so much of a decedent's things that it interferes with some other transfers. To avoid a spouse wanting to use the Elective Share most people give over 1/2 of their things to any spouse of theirs (including any family house).

YOUNG CHILD ISSUES

WILL CAN NAME A GUARDIAN TO CARE FOR YOUNG CHILD

If a parent dies with a child under age 18 then any other natural or adopted parent (but not a step-parent) almost always automatically gets control of the child's care (including health care, school, and home issues). This won't occur only if the other parent will be unavailable a long time or is proven unfit in court which is rare. But just in case it is later needed (like later both parents die) a Will often names a healthy willing relative or friend as "Guardian" to give this care for a young child. Many states call this a "Guardian of the Person".

WILL CAN NAME A CONSERVATOR FOR CHILD'S MONEY AND PROPERTY

Since a child until age 18 can't legally easily control property and money a Will often names a person to be "Conservator" to have the job of managing a young child's property and money. Many states call this a "Guardian of the Estate". This person decides each year how to use property and money on a child's needs (like on school, living, and health care) and then usually at age 18 anything left goes to the child. A person paying things for a child can ask to be paid back by a Conservator. Judges may hold a yearly hearing on spending. As a nice 2nd option to avoid work and costs most Wills say an Executor may name a person including themselves as "Custodian" to handle things under the new Uniform Transfers To Minors Act law.

MOST WILLS NAME 1 PERSON TO CARE FOR CHILD AND THEIR PROPERTY

This book's Will forms and most parents name the same 1 person to be Guardian caring for a child and Conservator caring for a child's property and money. People can change a Will to name different people for the 2 positions, but this is rarely worth it since parents dying is rare, rarely do children get much, a person smart enough to handle a child often can handle money, and naming different people can lead to arguments and lawsuits between people. Will gifts can go to someone named to be a Guardian or Conservator.

PERSON TO HELP A CHILD MUST BE AT LEAST 21

To serve and help a child in Colorado a person must be at least age 21 but they needn't reside in the state. Later usually a judge can't think they are unfit to serve, which usually means no serious criminal felony or a history of abuse or fraud. The choice by the last living parent is usually followed. If no Will names a person or they're unavailable a judge can pick someone, but family may argue about who to suggest. Naming 2 people to act at the same time is rare since 2 persons may argue and any 1 person named should be smart enough to act alone. In rare cases a married couple is named for the same position but then there can be problems if they divorce or disagree. Some Wills add a 2nd person to serve if the 1st person is unavailable, like: "or if they are later unable to serve I name _____ to serve"). But most people skip naming a fallback person since it is rarely needed, if a problem is seen a Will can be redone, and a judge can always pick someone.

NAMING PERSONS TO HELP CHILD RARELY MATTERS

A child under age 18 having parents die is rare so parents shouldn't worry that much about naming people to help a child. A good U.S. study found of people under age 18 just 2.78% had lost 1 parent and just 0.13% had lost 2 parents (so 99.87% of children by the time they reach age 18 will not lose both parents). *Parent Mortality Census SIPP Paper #288.*

CHAPTER 6
BASIC IDEAS ABOUT CONTROLLING HEALTH CARE

SOME BASIC IDEAS HELP UNDERSTANDING OF HEALTH CARE LEGAL FORMS

Some ideas help people understand health care forms.

■ By law people controls their own health care by telling medical personnel what they want <u>unless they are "incapacitated"</u> by insufficient ability to a) <u>communicate</u> verbally or by notes, b) be <u>rational</u>, or c) be <u>conscious</u>. Most people keep control of their own care till death or till no big treatment options remain, but some people worry they may be incapacitated a long time so want to do health care forms.

■ Legal documents that help control health care are usually called "Advanced Directives".

■ If an adult 18 or older becomes incapacitated <u>the adult's closest family like spouse or adult child usually can make emergency decisions</u>. But later they usually must then rush to a judge to get further power if no legal document gives them more power over health care.

■ In legal documents a <u>person can be named to have control of health care</u> if needed. This person is often called the "Health Care Agent", "Health Care Attorney-in-Fact", "Health Care Advocate", or a similar name.

■ In legal documents people can <u>write medical instructions that doctors, family, and other people must obey</u>.

■ Parents even without legal documents mostly have <u>full</u> power over health care of <u>children under age 18</u>, and the only exception is teens have some freedom to pick their own family planning or gender related care.

■ Some <u>married people</u> do documents to give a spouse power over medical care if they are incapacitated. Some adults especially <u>to age 25</u> do documents to give this power to parents. The young are less often sick.

■ Pain relief like pain drugs or comfort care is still given even if documents say to stop or limit other care.

■ <u>Most people only do 1 legal document</u> about health care that often names someone to control health care if needed and has a spot for basic instructions (this is sometimes called a "Health Care Power of Attorney").

■ For the rare times stopping health care seems more likely to matter (like due to extreme illness or old age):

-- most people do nothing special and trust family or Health Care Agent to wisely decide when to stop care (they can weigh many factors like pain, cost, likely difficulty of treatment, beliefs, and chances of recovery);

-- a few people do a serious document to say to stop most health care if <u>later</u> doctors think an incapacitated person has very bad health and more medical care likely won't help (sometimes this is called a "Living Will";

-- a few people do a serious document to say <u>starting immediately</u> to not give most medical care (often this is called a "Do-Not-Resuscitate" if about resuscitation, or called a "Physician's Order" if about many treatments).

CHAPTER 7
FORM 1: WILL (STANDARD)

FORM 1 IS A STANDARD WILL THAT IS FLEXIBLE BUT WITHOUT A GUARDIAN

Form 1 is a standard Will that is flexible and lets a person control many different things after their death. This form has no part about a Guardian so this form is for a person with no child under age 18.

THIS FORM IS A WILL WITH SEVERAL PARTS

The form starts with lines for a person to put their name (a full legal name is best but not required) and place of main residence (most put a county but some put a city). The Will is still valid if people later move.

Paragraph 1, "List Of Spouse And Children", lets a person write the names of any living spouse and children they have, or if none maybe write "none". This helps show a Testator has enough mental ability and memory to do a Will. Not listing a living spouse or child here can let an omitted person ask a judge to give them a share or all of a Testator's property and money by claiming they were accidently forgotten.

Paragraph 2, "Gifts", has many spaces to make either specific gifts of particular property or general gifts like of money. People can delete, copy and paste to add more, or leave blank these gift lines.

Paragraph 3, "Separate Writings", says to follow any separate writings done apart from the Will that gifts tangible personal property in manner allowed by state law.

Paragraph 4, "Residue", has a Residue Clause to say property and money left after other Will parts and other transfers is to be distributed in the way a person wrote in the blank parts of this paragraph.

Paragraph 5, "Administration", names a person to be Personal Representative to do things after a person's death (in the past the similar term Executor was used in Colorado for the person doing this).

Paragraph 6, "Miscellaneous", has paragraphs of legal language to help avoid certain legal issues.

Last is paragraphs for Testator to print their name and the date and then sign, and for the 2 witnesses to print their name and addresses and then sign.

USUAL RESIDUE CLAUSE HAS 2 PLACES TO NAME PERSONS TO GET THINGS

In a Will "Residue Clause" anything left over after other Will parts is transferred as the clause directs. Many people use a Residue Clause to gift most their things. In this Will form's Residue Clause there is:

1) a 1st space to name 1 or more persons to get the Residue, and if any named here have died before the Will maker then other persons named here in this 1st space take the dead person's share, and

2) a 2nd space to name people to get things if all people named in the 1st space have died, and if any people named in the 2nd space have died their shares go to "lineal descendants" like their children.

People often put in the 1st space a spouse or closest family or friends, and in 2nd space next closest people.

TESTATOR AND 2 WITNESSES WHILE TOGETHER SIGN WILL

This Will after being filled out (except bits intentionally left blank) must be signed by the person doing the Will (the "Testator") in front of at least 2 persons acting as witnesses at least age 18 who then also sign.

LAST WILL AND TESTAMENT

I am _____ of _____, Colorado, and I revoke all prior Wills and testamentary documents and do make, publish, and declare this as my Will. I am now of sound mind and under no duress or undue influence and acting voluntarily.

1. LIST OF SPOUSE AND CHILDREN. To help show I am mentally competent and have sufficient memory to make a Will I wish to list any living spouse and living children I now have. I currently have the following living spouse and living children:
_____
_____.

2. GIFTS. I give these gifts in this Will, but to get a gift in this section the recipient must survive me except as otherwise stated below.

I give _____ to _____.
I give _____ to _____.
I give _____ to _____.
I give _____ to _____.
I give _____ to _____.
I give _____ to _____.
I give _____ to _____.
I give _____ to _____.

3. SEPARATE WRITINGS. I may do writings separate from this Will to gift tangible personal property as allowed by state law, and all such writings should be followed. But any such writing not found within 90 days of my death is canceled and has no effect. A gift in such a writing to a person who does not survive me is canceled and has no effect. This Will does not revoke any such writings that now exist.

4. RESIDUE. I give the rest and residue and remainder of my estate, my money and property of any kind and nature, and anything I have an interest in so long as it was not transferred by other Will provisions (all of which is called the "residue"), as follows:
  a) to _____ who survive me with persons just named who survive me taking the share of non-survivors, then if anything remains
  b) to _____ and if any of those just named do not survive me their part goes to their lineal descendants per stirpes.

5. ADMINISTRATION. I name, nominate, and appoint _____ as Personal Representative including for me, my Will, and my estate.

6. MISCELLANEOUS. The following applies to this Will and generally.

In this Will no part left unfilled is a mistake including spaces in the residue clause.

The facts support and I want Colorado state law to apply to this Will and my estate.

I order that my just debts, funeral and related expenses, and taxes be paid as soon after my death as practical but only those items my Personal Representative chooses to pay.

Priority of Will gifts of the same type is based on the order they are written.

The words "give" and "gift" also means a devise, bequest, grant, legacy, or similar.

I am intentionally not providing by Will or other ways for some family, including I am not providing for some children of mine and also children of a deceased child of mine.

If a gift Will reasonably mentions survival then survival is an absolute condition and anti-lapse laws or similar provisions have no effect and without survival the gift lapses. Unless a Will gift specifies otherwise if a Will gift goes to multiple recipients if any do not survive me the part to them lapses and instead goes to other surviving recipients.

No earlier transfer reduces a Will gift unless I usually called it a loan or advancement.

Unless another meaning is shown use of plural includes the singular and vice versa, and "they" can mean 1 person. Masculine, feminine, and neuter words are interchangeable.

Unless a Will specifically says otherwise a secured debt including a mortgage or lien shall not be paid off including by a Personal Representative or in probate, and a recipient of a Will gift of property takes it subject to debts. Also, no recipient of property who may lose it or who pays to keep it may have my estate or others pay or do exoneration.

If during my life I disposed of an item in a specific gift then the gift is extinguished.

I request and authorize any informal, summary, and quick probate or similar action. Any Personal Representative may act independently with no supervision of any court, including independent administration, and with no inventory, appraisal, or other action.

I give any Personal Representative the a) fullest authority, discretion, and powers allowed by state law, b) power to lease, sell, mortgage, convey, or keep property including real property in a manner and time they deem helpful or proper, and c) authority to settle or pay claims or debts in the time and manner they in their sole discretion choose.

A Personal Representative may request and be paid reasonable compensation.

Any Guardian of any type, Conservator, Custodian, or other person managing a minor's property or money may use or invade the principal and sell property without court action.

If context permits the terms Personal Representative and Executor and Administrator are interchangeable, Conservator and Guardian of the Estate and Guardian of Property and Custodian are interchangeable, and residue and residuary are interchangeable. Any such person may stand in the place of and have all powers like the others named here.

The residue includes lapsed or failed gifts, insurance paid to the estate, digital assets, inheritances owed me, and all I had power of appointment or testamentary disposition over.

Any Personal Representative, Executor, Administrator, Guardian of any type like for a person or estate, Conservator, Custodian, and any other fiduciary under this Will or otherwise shall qualify and serve without bond, surety, security, surety bond, or similar.

If evidence does not show it likely a person survived me by 120 hours (5 days) then for this Will and my estate they shall be deemed in all ways as having died before me.

If part of this Will is by law invalid or unenforceable other provisions remain in effect.

Any Personal Representative may at any time transfer money or property of a minor under age 18 to a Custodian to serve under the Colorado Uniform Transfers to Minors Act or a similar law anywhere, and may pick the person to be Custodian including themselves.

TESTATOR

IN WITNESS WHEREOF, I, _____, the Testator, declare that this instrument is my Will which I make as Testator, that I do this as a free and voluntary act for the purposes expressed therein, that I am at least 18 years of age and of sound mind and under no constraint or undue influence, and that I do sign this instrument voluntarily as my Will in the presence and sight of each of the two persons who witness this Will who are named and who sign below, this _____ day of _____, 20____.

_____
Testator signature

WITNESSES

We, _____ and _____, the Witnesses, sign our names to this instrument, and do hereby declare to everyone (including any undersigned authority to which we may have been sworn) that the Testator signs and executes this instrument as the Will of the Testator and that the Testator signs it willingly, and that the Testator executes it as the Testator's free and voluntary act for the purposes therein expressed, and that each of us, in the conscious presence of the Testator, hereby at Testator's request signs this Will to witness the Testator's signing, and that to the best of our knowledge the Testator is 18 years of age or older, of sound mind, and under no constraint or undue influence.

_____ _____
Witness #1 signature   Witness #1 address

_____ _____
Witness #2 signature   Witness #2 address

CHAPTER 8
FORM 2: WILL (GUARDIAN)

FORM 2 IS A WILL WITH GUARDIAN PART FOR PEOPLE WITH A YOUNG CHILD

Form 2 is a Will with a Guardian part to be used by a person with a minor child under age 18.

FORM IS A WILL WITH SEVERAL PARTS INCLUDING A GUARDIAN PART

The form starts with lines for a person to put their name (a full legal name is best but not required) and place of main residence (most put a county but some put a city). The Will is still valid if people later move.

Paragraph 1, "List Of Spouse And Children", lets a person write the names of any living spouse and children they have, or if none maybe write "none". This helps show a Testator has enough mental ability and memory to do a Will. Not listing a living spouse or child here can let an omitted person ask a judge to give them a share or all of a Testator's property and money by claiming they were accidently forgotten.

Paragraph 2, "Gifts", has many spaces to make either specific gifts of particular property or general gifts like of money. People can delete, copy and paste to add more, or leave blank these gift lines.

Paragraph 3, "Separate Writings", says to follow any separate writings done apart from the Will that gifts tangible personal property in manner allowed by state law.

Paragraph 4, "Residue", has a Residue Clause to say property and money left after other Will parts and other transfers is to be distributed in the way a person wrote in the blank parts of this paragraph.

Paragraph 5, "Administration", names a person to be Personal Representative to do things after a person's death (in the past the similar term Executor was used in Colorado for the person doing this).

Paragraph 6, "Guardian", names a person to if needed be Guardian to care for any minor child under age 18 (like if both parents die) and be Conservator to if needed manage a child's property and money.

Paragraph 7, "Miscellaneous", has paragraphs of legal language to help avoid certain legal issues.

Last is paragraphs for Testator to print their name and the date and then sign, and for the 2 witnesses to print their name and addresses and then sign.

USUAL RESIDUE CLAUSE HAS 2 PLACES TO NAME PERSONS TO GET THINGS

In a Will "Residue Clause" anything left over after other Will parts is transferred as the clause directs. Many people use a Residue Clause to gift most their things. In this Will form's Residue Clause there is:

1) a 1st space to name 1 or more persons to get the Residue, and if any named here have died before the Will maker then other persons named here in this 1st space take the dead person's share, and

2) a 2nd space to name people to get things if all people named in the 1st space have died, and if any people named in the 2nd space have died their shares go to "lineal descendants" like their children.

People often put in the 1st space a spouse or closest family or friends, and in 2nd space next closest people.

TESTATOR AND 2 WITNESSES WHILE TOGETHER SIGN WILL

This Will after being filled out (except bits intentionally left blank) must be signed by the person doing the Will (the "Testator") in front of at least 2 persons acting as witnesses at least age 18 who then also sign.

LAST WILL AND TESTAMENT

I am _____ of _____, Colorado, and I revoke all prior Wills and testamentary documents and do make, publish, and declare this as my Will. I am now of sound mind and under no duress or undue influence and acting voluntarily.

1. LIST OF SPOUSE AND CHILDREN. To help show I am mentally competent and have sufficient memory to make a Will I wish to list any living spouse and living children I now have. I currently have the following living spouse and living children:

_____

_____.

2. GIFTS. I give these gifts in this Will, but to get a gift in this section the recipient must survive me except as otherwise stated below.

I give _____ to _____.

I give _____ to _____.

I give _____ to _____.

I give _____ to _____.

I give _____ to _____.

I give _____ to _____.

3. SEPARATE WRITINGS. I may do writings separate from this Will to gift tangible personal property as allowed by state law, and all such writings should be followed. But any such writing not found within 90 days of my death is canceled and has no effect. A gift in such a writing to a person who does not survive me is canceled and has no effect. This Will does not revoke any such writings that now exist.

4. RESIDUE. I give the rest and residue and remainder of my estate, my money and property of any kind and nature, and anything I have an interest in so long as it was not transferred by other Will provisions (all of which is called the "residue"), as follows:

    a) to _____ who survive me with persons just named who survive me taking the share of non-survivors, then if anything remains

    b) to _____ and if any of those just named do not survive me their part goes to their lineal descendants per stirpes.

5. ADMINISTRATION. I name, nominate, and appoint _____ as Personal Representative including for me, my Will, and my estate.

6. GUARDIAN. I name, nominate, and appoint _____
to be Guardian of any minor child of mine and also to have care, authority, custody, and other control of them (including as Guardian of the Person). I also name this same person to be Conservator for any minor child of mine and also to have care, control, and power over their property, money, and estate (including as Guardian of the Estate).

7. MISCELLANEOUS. The following applies to this Will and generally.
   In this Will no part left unfilled is a mistake including spaces in the residue clause.
   The facts support and I want Colorado state law to apply to this Will and my estate.
   I order that my just debts, funeral and related expenses, and taxes be paid as soon after my death as practical but only those items my Personal Representative chooses to pay.
   Priority of Will gifts of the same type is based on the order they are written.
   The words "give" and "gift" also means a devise, bequest, grant, legacy, or similar.
   I am intentionally not providing by Will or other ways for some family, including I am not providing for some children of mine and also children of a deceased child of mine.
   If a gift Will reasonably mentions survival then survival is an absolute condition and anti-lapse laws or similar provisions have no effect and without survival the gift lapses. Unless a Will gift specifies otherwise if a Will gift goes to multiple recipients if any do not survive me the part to them lapses and instead goes to other surviving recipients.
   No earlier transfer reduces a Will gift unless I usually called it a loan or advancement.
   Unless another meaning is shown use of plural includes the singular and vice versa, and "they" can mean 1 person. Masculine, feminine, and neuter words are interchangeable.
   Unless a Will specifically says otherwise a secured debt including a mortgage or lien shall not be paid off including by a Personal Representative or in probate, and a recipient of a Will gift of property takes it subject to debts. Also, no recipient of property who may lose it or who pays to keep it may have my estate or others pay or do exoneration.
   If during my life I disposed of an item in a specific gift then the gift is extinguished.
   I request and authorize any informal, summary, and quick probate or similar action. Any Personal Representative may act independently with no supervision of any court, including independent administration, and with no inventory, appraisal, or other action.
   I give any Personal Representative the a) fullest authority, discretion, and powers allowed by state law, b) power to lease, sell, mortgage, convey, or keep property including real property in a manner and time they deem helpful or proper, and c) authority to settle or pay claims or debts in the time and manner they in their sole discretion choose.
   A Personal Representative may request and be paid reasonable compensation.
   Any Guardian of any type, Conservator, Custodian, or other person managing a minor's property or money may use or invade the principal and sell property without court action.
   If context permits the terms Personal Representative and Executor and Administrator are interchangeable, Conservator and Guardian of the Estate and Guardian of Property and Custodian are interchangeable, and residue and residuary are interchangeable. Any such person may stand in the place of and have all powers like the others named here.

The residue includes lapsed or failed gifts, insurance paid to the estate, digital assets, inheritances owed me, and all I had power of appointment or testamentary disposition over.

Any Personal Representative, Executor, Administrator, Guardian of any type like for a person or estate, Conservator, Custodian, and any other fiduciary under this Will or otherwise shall qualify and serve without bond, surety, security, surety bond, or similar.

If evidence does not show it likely a person survived me by 120 hours (5 days) then for this Will and my estate they shall be deemed in all ways as having died before me.

If part of this Will is by law invalid or unenforceable other provisions remain in effect.

Any Personal Representative may at any time transfer money or property of a minor under age 18 to a Custodian to serve under the Colorado Uniform Transfers to Minors Act or a similar law anywhere, and may pick the person to be Custodian including themselves.

TESTATOR

IN WITNESS WHEREOF, I, _____, the Testator, declare that this instrument is my Will which I make as Testator, that I do this as a free and voluntary act for the purposes expressed therein, that I am at least 18 years of age and of sound mind and under no constraint or undue influence, and that I do sign this instrument voluntarily as my Will in the presence and sight of each of the two persons who witness this Will who are named and who sign below, this _____ day of _____, 20____.

_____
Testator signature

WITNESSES

We, _____ and _____, the Witnesses, sign our names to this instrument, and do hereby declare to everyone (including any undersigned authority to which we may have been sworn) that the Testator signs and executes this instrument as the Will of the Testator and that the Testator signs it willingly, and that the Testator executes it as the Testator's free and voluntary act for the purposes therein expressed, and that each of us, in the conscious presence of the Testator, hereby at Testator's request signs this Will to witness the Testator's signing, and that to the best of our knowledge the Testator is 18 years of age or older, of sound mind, and under no constraint or undue influence.

_____ _____
Witness #1 signature   Witness #1 address

_____ _____
Witness #2 signature   Witness #2 address

CHAPTER 9
FORM 3: SELF-PROVING AFFIDAVIT

FORM CAN BE DONE TO MAKE USING A WILL LATER A BIT EASIER

This form is optional but can be done after a Will is done to help reduce later legal work after a death. This is a statutory form.

FORM SAVES LATER WORK OF SHOWING WILL WAS PROPERLY SIGNED

A Self-Proving Affidavit "proves" a Will was signed properly. If this form is not done then after death a little work is need to get evidence from either witnesses to the Will signing, persons familiar with the signatures of people, or a handwriting expert. If this form is not done there is a bit more legal risk a Will won't be followed later. But of people doing Wills about <u>half skip a Self-Proving Affidavit</u> mostly due to hassle of finding a notary on top of 2 witnesses each time a Will is done or re-done, and since it mostly just saves a little later work of people who are happy to do work while getting property and money through a Will. Colorado has a Self-Proving Affidavit form but several states have no similar form and manage fine.

FORM IS DONE BY TESTATOR AND 2 WITNESSES SIGNING BEFORE NOTARY

For this form to be valid a person who is a notary (also called a "notary public") must see the Testator and 2 witnesses sign and then the notary notarizes it. A notary can be found and politely asked to help at a bank, insurance agent, government office, or by looking in a phonebook. A notary is likelier to help if a person is an existing customer or pays. This form is often done a few minutes after a Will is signed but it can be done much later (even years later) when everyone can meet with a notary. This form can't legally be done before a Will is done. This form when done is often kept paper-clipped to the Will it supports.

SELF-PROVING AFFIDAVIT

(Colorado Revised Statutes § 15-11-504 (2))

THE STATE OF COLORADO

COUNTY OF _____

    We, _____, _____, and _____, the Testator and the Witnesses, respectively, whose names are signed to the attached or foregoing instrument, being first duly sworn, do hereby declare to the undersigned authority that the Testator signed and executed the instrument as the Testator's Will and that the Testator had signed willingly (or willingly directed another to sign for the Testator), and that the Testator executed it as Testator's free and voluntary act for the purposes therein expressed, and that each of the Witnesses, in the conscious presence of the Testator, signed the Will acting as a witness and that to the best of the knowledge of all Witnesses the Testator was at that time 18 years of age or older, of sound mind, and under no constraint or undue influence.

_____
Testator

_____   _____
Witness   Witness

Subscribed, sworn to, and acknowledged before me by _____, the Testator, and subscribed and sworn to before me by _____ and _____, Witnesses, this _____ day of _____, 20 _____.

    (SEAL, if any)

                                  (SIGNED) _____
                                  (Official capacity of officer) _____

CHAPTER 10
FORM 4: TANGIBLE PERSONAL PROPERTY MEMORANDUM

FORM LETS PROPERTY GIFTS TO OCCUR AT DEATH BE ADDED OUTSIDE WILL
This form lets people write to add some more gifts of property they want to occur after death. This form is often called by people a memo, list, or statement.

FORM GIVES EASY QUICK WAY TO WRITE MORE GIFTS OF PROPERTY
This form lets a person easily write some more gifts of property to occur at their death without having to re-write a Will. To use this form Colorado law requires a valid Will says that it can be used, and all this book's Will forms say this. If this form and a Will gift the very same item then by law the Will is followed. If more than 1 of these forms gift the same item then the more recently done page controls. People can modify an existing form page if they put a new date and signature on it. Note, to try to help avoid later delay this book's form says any of these forms not found within 90 days of a death will be ignored.

FORM CAN ONLY GIFT TANGIBLE PERSONAL PROPERTY
Under Colorado law this form can only gift "tangible personal property". This means property that is tangible (touchable), so not accounts or moneys or investments related to papers, banks, or some entity like a corporation or partnership or trust. This also means property that is personal property, so not real property (land or buildings) and not fixtures (anything buried or tied to land). The form can't gift money whether coin or paper currency, even if it's an antique or foreign money. Most lawyers recommend people not use the form to give items used in a trade or business. Improper property written in the form is later just ignored. This form is often used to gift clothes, furniture, vehicles, tools, building supplies, antiques, electronics, art, appliances, and jewelry.

It may help understanding to show the Colorado law allowing this form, which in its main part says:

15-11-513. Separate writing or memorandum identifying devise of certain types of tangible personal property.

[A] will may refer to a written statement or list to dispose of items of tangible personal property not otherwise specifically disposed of by the will, other than money.

To be admissible under this section as evidence of the intended disposition, the writing shall be either in the handwriting of the testator or be signed by the testator and shall describe the items and the devisees with reasonable certainty.

The writing may be referred to as one to be in existence at the time of the testator's death; it may be prepared before or after the execution of the will; it may be altered by the testator after its preparation; and it may be a writing that has no significance apart from its effect on the dispositions made by the will.

TO COMPLETE THE FORM A PERSON JUST SIGNS AND DATES IT
This form to be legally valid just must be signed and usually dated by the person who is doing the form. Once completed this form is often kept with a Will. To cancel this form it can be destroyed, crossed out, or just thrown away so it is not found later.

TANGIBLE PERSONAL PROPERTY MEMORANDUM

In this writing are gifts of tangible personal property to occur at my death, but this writing if not found by someone within 90 days of my death is canceled.

I may do many pages of these writings which should all be seen as one document. If there are conflicts among such writings the provisions of the more recent writing will revoke the inconsistent provisions of a prior writing.

If a person getting a gift below does not survive me such gift is void and canceled.

DESCRIPTION OF PROPERTY   NAMES OF RECIPIENTS

_____ to _____

_____ to _____

_____ to _____

_____ to _____

_____ to _____

_____ to _____

_____ to _____

_____ to _____

_____ to _____

_____ to _____

_____ to _____

_____ to _____

_____ to _____

_____ to _____

_____ to _____

_____ to _____

Date:_____ Signed:_____

CHAPTER 11
FORM 5: HANDWRITTEN WILL

WILL CAN SKIP USING THE NORMAL 2 WITNESSES IF IT'S ALL HANDWRITTEN

A Handwritten Will is a Will that is easier to do since in Colorado it does not need the usual 2 witnesses if it is completely handwritten by the person doing the Will.

HANDWRITTEN WILL WITHOUT WITNESSES IS ALLOWED IN COLORADO

In 27 states including Colorado a person doing a Will can skip having the usual 2 witnesses for a Will if: 1) it is all handwritten by the person doing the Will (not photocopied, typed, computer printed, or handwritten by anyone else), and 2) it is signed and dated. Many people call this a Handwritten Will and lawyers call it a Holographic Will (Holo means Whole and Graph means Image in the Greek language). Colorado politicians allow this since handwriting is harder to fake, people may be in an emergency or rush, witnesses may be scarce in the countryside, it is private, it can be cheap by skipping complexity and people, and it is traditional to do this especially in rural places. The 27 states that allow Handwritten Wills have about 55% of the U.S. population so these Handwritten Wills are used in many places and familiar to many judges and lawyers. See states with Handwritten Wills on map below in dark.

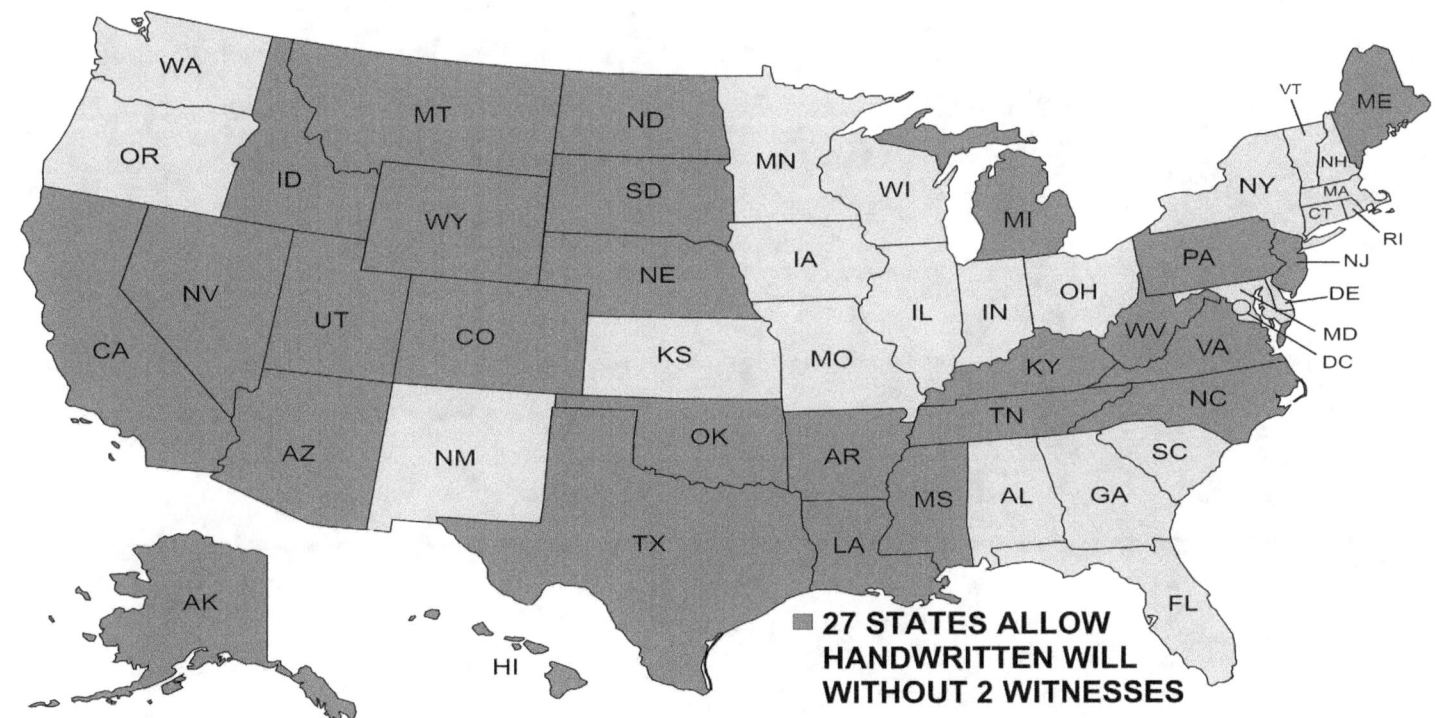

HANDWRITTEN WILLS ARE USUALLY FINE BUT REQUIRE LATER WORK

Some lawyers warn against Handwritten Wills saying they often read confusingly, skip legal words that help in some cases, and are found invalid more often – but some studies show they are liked and usually fine. To use a Handwritten Will later after a death some people must in writing or in testimony say the handwriting looks like the Testator's, which can be a hassle. But a normal Will if no Self-Proving Affidavit was done also needs similar proof like from a witness to the signing or other proof of signing. Handwritten Wills tend to be done by people who are young so unlikely to need a Will soon, who are in a hurry, who want to fix a mistake, who before a trip want to pick a Guardian, who moved to a new state, or who plan to do a better Will later.

WORDS BELOW ON THIS PAGE CAN BE USED FOR A HANDWRITTEN WILL

People can do a Handwritten Will in a sentence that is legal but may leave out helpful parts, for example: *"As my Will I give my estate and all else to Ann Baker who shall be Executor. - Dan Baker"*
But it is recommended people <u>use more complex words for a Handwritten Will shown on this page below</u>.
To do this people should change the names and words below on this page to match what they want done.
<u>If some people named to get things later die it is usually best to re-do the Will and name different people.</u>
The last paragraph about Guardians for children can be skipped if a person has no children under age 18.
This Will must be all handwritten by the person doing it on some paper (pencil or pen is fine) and then signed and dated by the person (usually in pen or permanent marker).

WILL

1. I am John David Baker and I currently live in Weld County, Colorado. I revoke any prior Wills and Codicils and declare this to be my Will.

2. I give my estate, property, money, and other things to Jane Eve Baker and Wendy Sue Hill. My not giving to some family is intentional.

3. I name Jane Eve Baker as Personal Representative for me, my Will, and my estate. I request informal probate.

4. No bond or similar is needed of any Personal Representative, Guardian, or Conservator.

5. If ever needed for a minor child of mine I name Mary Ann Dodd as Guardian to have care, custody, and control of them, and I name this same person as Conservator with control and power over any minor's property, money, and estate.

May 8, 2024   *John David Baker*

CHAPTER 12
FORM 6: MEDICAL DURABLE POWER OF ATTORNEY

FORM CAN NAME HEALTH CARE AGENT AND GIVE INSTRUCTIONS

This form lets a person in case it's needed later name someone to be Health Care Agent to make decisions and, also, lets a person give health care instructions. Many people do this 1 form and skip all similar health care forms. This form mostly matters only if a person is later incapacitated by a substantial inability to communicate verbally or in writing, inability to think rationally, or inability to stay conscious. This form takes a long time to read and is not usually followed by paramedics and other persons in a hurry.

PERSON CAN NAME AN AGENT TO SHARE POWER OVER HEALTH CARE

This form lets someone be named as Agent to have power to talk to health personnel and make medical decisions for person who did the form. Often named as Agent is a spouse, relative, or a trusted good friend. Sometimes this person is called a Health Care Attorney-in-Fact. The Agent should then do what the person would probably want, obey written instructions, and obey any verbal instructions clearly made to them. This form is called "durable" which means valid even if person is later incapacitated. Having an Agent while a person is just a bit sick or tired can help by letting a person rest while the Agent makes minor decisions. A person with capacity and still thinking well can always over-rule their Agent or fire them from the position by saying this clearly to them and usually to doctors.

FORM CAN GIVE HEALTH CARE INSTRUCTIONS

In the form a person can give written health care instructions that family, Agent, and doctors must all legally follow. But many people skip written instructions since they are hard to write to cover all situations, they can cause legal delay and problems if not totally clear, and people even without instructions trust the judgment of an Agent or family. In the form a person people can name an Agent but skip instructions, or can do instructions and skip an Agent.

MUST SIGN FORM AND USING WITNESSES AND NOTARY IS COMMON

Colorado law is flexible and legally the form can be completed just by signing, but it is standard to also involve either 2 witnesses or a notary (especially if the form might be used out of state). A person should use witnesses who are at least age 18, not named Agent in the form, not workers or doctors involved in giving health care to the person, and preferably not someone who may inherit or financially benefit from the person's death. Often witnesses are friends, family, a hospital worker not giving care, or just strangers. Once done the form should be quickly shown to all places that may provide health care so it can be made part of the person's medical file and followed. Many people also keep the form handy so they or their family can show it if needed. To cancel this form a person can clearly tell the Agent it is canceled and take back copies and also maybe tell all places that saw the form that it is canceled.

MEDICAL DURABLE POWER OF ATTORNEY

1. APPOINTMENT OF AGENT AND OPTIONAL ALTERNATE
I, _____, the person doing this document as the Declarant, hereby appoint:
_____
(name, address, email, phone)

as my Agent to make and communicate my healthcare decisions when I cannot. I give my Agent power to consent to or refuse or stop any healthcare, treatment, service, or diagnostic procedure. I give my Agent power to fill out and sign documents and apply for and act in writing for insurance, admission to any facility, applying for benefits, or handling payment. This Power of Attorney shall not be affected by my subsequent disability or incapacity. My Agent also has authority to talk with healthcare personnel, get information, and sign forms as necessary to carry out those decisions, and should be treated as I would with respect to use, disclosure, and other actions involving my individually identifiable health information and other medical records (including I give authority to access, receive and request all information governed by HIPAA and similar laws.

(Optional) Although not required to do so, if the person named above is unavailable or unable to continue as Agent then I appoint the following person as Agent to do as described above:
_____
(name, address, email, phone)

2. WHEN THIS DOCUMENT TAKES EFFECT
By this document I am creating a Medical Durable Power of Attorney which takes effect either (initial one):
_____ (Initials) When my physician determines I am unable to make or express my own decisions, and for as long as I am unable to make or express my own decisions.
_____ (Initials) Immediately upon my signature.

3. INSTRUCTIONS TO AGENT
Although not required I know I can give instructions to my Agent that must be followed, doing so either in this document or in another way at anytime. Except about things I have given instructions my Agent may decide for themselves about healthcare decisions for me. I do now give some instructions (optional):
_____
_____

4. COMPLETION OF THIS DOCUMENT
Below is the signature of Declarant to complete this document. Using two witnesses or a notary is **not** required by Colorado law but is common to encourage people to follow this document especially in other states.

Date:_____   Signature of Declarant: _____

We, the Witnesses, do declare: this document was signed by _____ (name of Declarant) in our presence, and we who are at least 18 years old and in the presence of each other and at Declarant's request sign as witnesses, and when signing the Declarant was of sound mind and under no pressure or undue influence.

Signature of Witness:_____
Address and Phone/Email of Witness:_____

Signature of Witness:_____
Address and Phone/Email of Witness:_____

Notary (optional)
State of _____, County of _____}
SUBSCRIBED and sworn to before me by _____, the Declarant, _____ and _____ witnesses, as the voluntary act and deed of the Declarant this _____ day of _____, 20__.

_____   My commission expires:_____
Notary Public

CHAPTER 13
FORM 7: LIVING WILL

FORM CAN SAY END TREATMENTS IF LATER DOCTORS THINK IT'S USELESS

This form lets a person say to stop certain health care if <u>later</u> doctors think the person is incapacitated and has an irrevocable terminal condition and further medical care likely won't help. Doing this form is very serious and usually only the sickest or oldest people do it. This form takes a long time to read and is <u>not</u> usually followed by paramedics and other persons in a hurry.

IN FORM CAN SAY NO TO FURTHER MEDICAL CARE WITH A FEW DETAILS

In the form a person can say to not give certain medical care if <u>later</u> doctors think it is very unlikely to help an incapacitated person. The language in the form explains how and when care might be stopped. The form has spots to say what care to stop, like whether to not give C.P.R. or not give food or water by tube. Doctors can help explain this form. Care that may be stopped in the form is often called "life-sustaining" which is different than "comfort care" which is pain medication and pain therapy that usually continues.

PEOPLE SHOULD SIGN FORM WITH TWO WITNESSES AND MAYBE A NOTARY

This form is signed by the person doing the form in front of 2 witnesses who also sign it. Also using a notary is optional but is often done to make a form more likely to be followed especially in other states. A person should use as witnesses some persons at least age 18, who are not named as Agent to control health care for the person, preferably people not involved in a person's healthcare, and preferably not a person who may inherit or financially benefit from a death. Often used as witnesses are family, friends, hospital workers not directly involved in care, or strangers. Once completed the form should be shown to all places that may provide health care so it can be made part of the person's medical file and followed. Many people also keep the form handy so they or their family can show it if needed. To cancel this form a person can clearly say aloud it is canceled and maybe tell all places that saw the form that it is canceled.

LIVING WILL

1. DECLARATION

I, _____, am at least age 18 and able to make and communicate my own decisions. I direct the following instructions if a) I am unable to make or communicate my decisions on about medical treatment and b) my physician and another qualified physician certify in writing I am in a terminal condition or persistent vegetative state.

   A. Life-Sustaining Procedures while in a terminal condition or persistent vegetative state (*initial one*):
   _____ (*Initials*) I direct all life-sustaining procedures shall be withdrawn and withheld (but not including procedures felt helpful by healthcare providers to provide comfort or relieve pain).
   _____ (*Initials*) I direct life-sustaining procedures shall be continued until the following timeframe and then stop (but not including procedures felt helpful by healthcare providers to provide comfort or relieve pain)(*state timeframe, for example "2 months" or "3 months at least, and continue if my spouse wishes" or "1 month then stop, unless I am in a terminal condition but likely will not remain being in a persistent vegetative state*): _____
   _____.
   _____ (*Initials*) I direct life-sustaining procedures be continued indefinitely, regardless of my prognosis.

   B. Artificial Nutrition and Hydration while in a terminal condition or persistent vegetative state (*initial one*):
   _____ (*Initials*) I direct all artificial nutrition and hydration shall not be continued.
   _____ (*Initials*) I direct artificial nutrition and hydration shall be continued for/until (*state timeframe*): _____.
   _____ (*Initials*) I direct artificial nutrition and hydration be continued indefinitely, regardless of my prognosis.

2. POWER OF MEDICAL POWER OF ATTORNEY (*initial one*)
_____ (*Initials*) My Agent under my Medical Durable Power of Attorney **shall** have the authority to override any of the directions stated here, whether I signed this declaration before or after I appointed that Agent.
_____ (*Initials*) My directions as stated here **may not** be overridden or revoked by my Agent under Medical Durable Power of Attorney, whether I signed this declaration before or after I appointed that Agent.

3. ANATOMICAL GIFTS
_____ (*Initials*) I **wish** to donate my (*check one or both*) _____ organs and/or _____ tissues, if medically possible.
_____ (*Initials*) I **do not wish** donate my organs or tissues.

4. SIGNATURE
I execute this declaration, as my free and voluntary act, this _____ day of _____, 20____.

_____
Declarant signature

VIII. DECLARATION OF WITNESSES
This declaration was signed by _____ (*name of Declarant*) in our presence, and we in the presence of each other and at the Declarant's request have signed below as witnesses. We declare when Declarant signed this declaration a) we believe he or she was of sound mind and under no pressure or undue influence, b) we are not doctors or employees of the attending doctor or healthcare facility caring for Declarant, c) we are not creditors or heirs of the Declarant and have no claim against any portion of the Declarant's estate, and d) we are 18 years of age or more, and under no pressure, undue influence, or otherwise disqualifying disability.

Signature of Witness   *Printed Name*   *Address*

_____

Signature of Witness   *Printed Name*   *Address*

_____

Notary (optional)
State of Colorado, County of _____}
SUBSCRIBED and sworn to before me by _____, the Declarant, _____ and _____ witnesses, as the voluntary act and deed of the Declarant this ____ day of _____, 20____.

_____   My commission expires:_____
Signature of Notary Public

CHAPTER 14
FORM 8: MEDICAL ORDERS FOR SCOPE OF TREATMENT

FORM CAN SAY TO IMMEDIATELY NO LONGER GIVE CERTAIN HEALTH CARE

The Medical Orders for Scope of Treatment form, which is often called the "M.O.S.T." form, says to immediately no longer try certain medical care. This is a serious action and usually only done by the very sickest or oldest people. The form is short and can be read fast (like by paramedics) and is often used outside a hospital or other facilities, but it can be used in these places too. This book's form is a standard form issued by the state. Most other states have a similar form.

IN FORM CAN PICK WHICH CARE TO IMMEDIATELY NO LONGER TRY

In the form a person can say what health care to immediately no longer try. For example, many people say to not try C.P.R. which is cardio-pulmonary resuscitation (which includes electric defibrillation) to attempt to restart or help breathing or the heart. Some people also say to not give food or water by artificial means. Doctors can explain the options and how to use the form which sometimes comes on bright green paper. Instead of this form some people in Colorado use the older and blue Directive To Withhold CPR form or a similar form that only covers C.P.R. Many people just call the M.O.S.T. form the Do-Not-Resuscitate form.

PERSON AND THEIR PHYSICIAN MUST SIGN DIRECTIVE FORM

The form must be signed by the person doing the form and their doctor (called in the form a "physician") or a similar professional. Once completed the form usually is shown to all places that may give health care so it can be put in a person's medical file and followed. Some people also keep copies handy for themselves or family to show to paramedics and others who want to give care. The form may be kept on a bedside table, on a home fridge, pinned to a shirt or in a pocket, or some people wear a special bracelet that doctors can help order. To cancel the form usually a person just tells all places that saw the form that it is canceled.

SEND ORIGINAL FORM WITH PERSON WHENEVER TRANSFERRED OR DISCHARGED

Colorado Medical Orders for Scope of Treatment (MOST)

- **FIRST** follow these orders, **THEN** contact Physician, Advanced Practice Nurse (APN), or Physician Assistant (PA) for further orders if indicated.
- These Medical Orders are based on the person's medical condition & wishes.
- If Section A or B is not completed, full treatment for that section is implied.
- May only be completed by, or on behalf of, a person 18 years of age or older.
- Everyone shall be treated with dignity and respect.

Legal Last Name		
Legal First Name/Middle Name		
Date of Birth		Sex
Hair Color	Eye Color	Race/Ethnicity

In preparing these orders, please inquire whether patient has executed a living will or other advance directive. If yes and available, review for consistency with these orders and update as needed. (See additional instructions on page 2.)

A — Check one box only
CARDIOPULMONARY RESUSCITATION (CPR)   ***Person has no pulse and is not breathing.***

☐ **Yes CPR:** Attempt Resuscitation   ☐ **No CPR:** Do Not Attempt Resuscitation

NOTE: Selecting 'Yes CPR' requires choosing "Full Treatment" in Section B. When _not_ in cardiopulmonary arrest, follow orders in Section B.

B — Check one box only
MEDICAL INTERVENTIONS   ***Person has pulse and/or is breathing.***

☐ **Full Treatment**—primary goal to prolong life by all medically effective means:
In addition to treatment described in Selective Treatment and Comfort-focused Treatment, use intubation, advanced airway interventions, mechanical ventilation, and cardioversion as indicated. Transfer to hospital if indicated. Includes intensive care.

☐ **Selective Treatment**—goal to treat medical conditions while avoiding burdensome measures:
In addition to treatment described in Comfort-focused Treatment below, use IV antibiotics and IV fluids as indicated. **Do not intubate.** May use noninvasive positive airway pressure. Transfer to hospital if indicated. **Avoid intensive care.**

☐ **Comfort-focused Treatment**—primary goal to maximize comfort:
Relieve pain and suffering with medication by any route as needed; use oxygen, suctioning, and manual treatment of airway obstruction. Do not use treatments listed in Full and Selective Treatment unless consistent with comfort goal. **Do not transfer to hospital for life-sustaining treatment. Transfer only if comfort needs cannot be met in current location.**

Additional Orders: _____

C — Check one box only
ARTIFICIALLY ADMINISTERED NUTRITION   *Always offer food & water by mouth if feasible.*

Any surrogate legal decision maker (Medical Durable Power of Attorney [MDPOA], Proxy-by-Statute, guardian, or other) must follow directions in the patient's living will, if any. Not completing this section **does not** imply any one of the choices—further discussion is required. NOTE: Special rules for Proxy-by-Statute apply; see reverse side ("Completing the MOST form") for details.

☐ Artificial nutrition by tube long term/permanent if indicated.
☐ Artificial nutrition by tube short term/temporary only. (May state term & goal in "Additional Orders")
☐ No artificial nutrition by tube.

Additional Orders: _____

D
DISCUSSED WITH (check all that apply):

☐ Patient
☐ Agent under Medical Durable Power of Attorney
☐ Proxy-by-Statute (per C.R.S. 15-18.5-103(6))
☐ Legal guardian
☐ Other: _____

SIGNATURES OF PROVIDER AND PATIENT, AGENT, GUARDIAN, OR PROXY-BY-STATUTE AND DATE (*MANDATORY*)

Significant thought has been given to these instructions. Preferences have been discussed and expressed to a healthcare professional. This document reflects those treatment preferences, which may also be documented in a Medical Durable Power OA, CPR Directive, living will, or other advance directive (attached if available). To the extent that previously completed advance directives do not conflict with these *Medical Orders for Scope of Treatment*, they shall remain in full force and effect.

If signed by surrogate legal decision maker, preferences expressed must reflect patient's wishes as best understood by surrogate.

Patient/Legal Decision Maker Signature (Mandatory)	Name (Print)	Relationship/ Decision maker status (Write "self" if patient)	Date Signed (Mandatory; Revokes all previous MOST forms)
Physician / APN / PA Signature (Mandatory)	Print Physician / APN / PA Name, Address, and Phone Number		Date Signed (Mandatory)
Colorado License #:			

HIPAA PERMITS DISCLOSURE OF THIS INFORMATION TO OTHER HEALTHCARE PROFESSIONALS AS NECESSARY

Authority for this form and process is granted by C.R.S. 15-18.7: Directives Concerning Medical Orders for Scope of Treatment, enacted 2010.

SEND ORIGINAL FORM WITH PERSON WHENEVER TRANSFERRED OR DISCHARGED

ADDITIONAL INFORMATION: *Please provide contact information below, in case follow up or more information needed.*

Patient Legal Last Name	Patient Legal First Name	Patient Middle Name (if any)	Patient Date of Birth

Primary Contact Person for the Patient	Relationship and/or MDPOA, Proxy, Guardian	Phone Number/email/Other contact information	

Healthcare Professional Preparing Form	Preparer Title	Phone Number/Email	Date Prepared

Patient Primary Diagnosis	Hospice Program (if applicable) /Address	Hospice Phone Number

DIRECTIONS FOR HEALTH CARE PROFESSIONALS

For more information, please refer to the "Getting the MOST Out of the Medical Orders for Scope of Treatment: Guidelines for Healthcare Professionals," www.ColoradoMOST.com

Completing the MOST form:
- MOST form master may be downloaded from www.ColoradoMOST.com and photocopied onto **Astrobrights® "Vulcan Green"** or **"Terra Green"** 60lb paper. This special paper is strongly encouraged but not required. Visit www.ColoradoMOST.com for a link to paper suppliers.
- The form must be signed by a physician, advanced practice nurse, or physician assistant to be valid as medical orders. Physician assistants must include physician name and contact information. In the absence of a provider signature, however, the patient selections should be considered as valid, documented patient preferences for treatment.
- Verbal orders are acceptable with follow-up signature by physician, advanced practice nurse, or physician assistant in accordance with facility policy, but not to exceed 30 days.
- **Completion of the MOST form is *not* mandatory.** "A healthcare facility shall not require a person to have executed a MOST form as a condition of being admitted to, or receiving medical treatment from, the healthcare facility" per C.R.S. 15-18.7-108.
- Patient preferences and medical indications shall guide the healthcare professional in completing the MOST form.
- Patients with capacity should participate in the discussion and sign these orders; a healthcare agent, Proxy-by-Statute, or guardian may complete these orders on behalf of an incapacitated patient, *making selections according to patient preferences, if known.*
- "Proxy-by-Statute" is a decision maker selected through a proxy process, per C.R.S. 15-18.5-103(6). Such a decision maker may not decline artificial nutrition or hydration (ANH) for an incapacitated patient without an attending physician and a second physician trained in neurology certifying that "the provision of ANH is merely prolonging the act of dying and is unlikely to result in the restoration of the patient to independent neurological functioning."
- **Photocopy, fax, and electronic images of signed MOST forms are legal and valid.**

Following the Medical Orders:
- Per C.R.S. 15-18.7-104: **Emergency medical personnel, a healthcare provider, or healthcare facility *shall* comply with an adult's properly executed MOST form that has been executed in this state or another state and is apparent and immediately available.** The fact that the signing physician, advanced practice nurse, or physician assistant does not have admitting privileges in the facility where the adult is receiving care does not remove the duty to comply with these orders. Providers who comply with the orders are immune from civil and criminal prosecution in connection with any outcome of complying with the orders.
- If a healthcare provider considers these orders *medically* inappropriate, she or he should discuss concerns with the patient or surrogate legal decision maker and revise orders only after obtaining the patient or surrogate consent.
- If Section A or B is not completed, full treatment is implied for that section.
- **Comfort care is never optional.** Among other comfort measures, oral fluids and nutrition must be offered if tolerated.
- When "Comfort-focused Treatment" is checked in Section B, hospice or palliative care referral is strongly recommended.
- If a healthcare provider or facility cannot comply with these orders due to policy or ethical/religious objections, the provider or facility must arrange to transfer the patient to another provider or facility and provide appropriate care until transfer.

Reviewing the Medical Orders:
- These medical orders should be reviewed
    - regularly by the person's attending physician or facility staff with the patient and/or patient's legal decision maker;
    - on admission to or discharge from any facility or on transfer between care settings or levels;
    - at any substantial change in the person's health status or treatment preferences; and
    - when legal decision maker or contact information changes.
- If substantive changes are made, please complete a new form and void the replaced one.
- **To void the form, draw a line across Sections A through C and write "VOID" in large letters. Sign and date.**

REVIEW OF THIS COLORADO MOST FORM

Review Date	Reviewer	Location of Review	Review Outcome
			☐ No Change ☐ New Form Completed
			☐ No Change ☐ New Form Completed
			☐ No Change ☐ New Form Completed
			☐ No Change ☐ New Form Completed

HIPAA PERMITS DISCLOSURE OF THIS INFORMATION TO OTHER HEALTHCARE PROFESSIONALS AS NECESSARY

Colorado Advance Directives Consortium, www.ColoradoMOST.com

CHAPTER 15
FORM 9: STATUTORY FORM POWER OF ATTORNEY

FORM LETS PERSON SHARE POWER OVER THEIR PROPERTY AND MONEY

This form lets a person share power with someone to let them do things with the person's money, property, debt, and more. Some people call this a "Financial Power of Attorney". This is a statutory form found at Colorado Revised Statutes § 15-14-741.

FORM GIVES POWER TO LET SOMEONE DO THINGS

This form lets a person share power to do things with their money, property, records, and other things with someone trusted like a spouse, other family member, or a friend. The person giving power is usually called the Principal, and the person getting power is usually called the Agent (or the Attorney in Fact). If a person is sick or busy this form can let someone help pay bills, use accounts, buy or sell items, borrow, hire workers, sign contracts, see records, and more. This form can avoid more serious legal options like a guardianship or conservatorship done through a court. Note, a person who isn't incapacitated can overrule or fire their Agent anytime. Importantly this form is usually "durable" which means it still is effective if the person who did the form is later incapacitated, but all power of the form ends at the person's death.

IN FORM POWERS GIVEN ARE INITIALED AND INSTRUCTIONS CAN BE GIVEN

In the form a person must initial to say which powers are given, or they can just initial the last item to give all the listed powers. Many people in the Grant Of General Authority section do give all these powers since if an Agent's power is not clear a bank, school, or other parties may hesitate or refuse to obey the Agent's orders. But most people do not give the powers in the later Grant Of Specific Authority section since these powers are less often needed and are riskier to give out. In the form a person can say who'd they prefer as Guardian or Conservator if a judge ever finds it needed, but many people don't bother with this.

DUE TO RISKS MANY SKIP THIS FORM OR CONSULT A LAWYER

Many people skip this form or first see a lawyer. Using this form is risky and can lead to harm since the Agent can be wasteful with money, commit fraud or theft, or by carelessness allow some other harms. A person acting as Agent has a duty to be loyal and act reasonably and can be sued for any harm, but they may later be out of money to pay. Usually banks and others can't be blamed for obeying an Agent's orders. The law is complex and basic acts of an Agent may be fine like paying bills but some acts may be improper like making gifts, risky investments, or unusual acts. It is best a person not the Agent do anything unusual.

PEOPLE SHOULD SIGN USUALLY WITH A NOTARY AND MAYBE 2 WITNESSES

In Colorado the form technically by law just needs to be signed and dated, but there is room for 2 witnesses and a notary, and most banks especially out of state won't follow the form if done with no notary. Witnesses if used should be at least 18, not named as Agent in the form, and preferably not close family. The signed form can be kept by a person until needed like due to illness, or given to the named Agent to hold and use. To cancel the form the person should tell the Agent and take back copies and also maybe tell all places that saw the form that it is canceled.

STATE OF COLORADO
STATUTORY FORM POWER OF ATTORNEY

IMPORTANT INFORMATION

This power of attorney authorizes another person (your agent) to make decisions concerning your property for you (the principal). Your agent will be able to make decisions and act with respect to your property (including your money) whether or not you are able to act for yourself. The meaning of authority over subjects listed on this form is explained in the "Uniform Power of Attorney Act", part 7 of article 14 of title 15, Colorado Revised Statutes.

This power of attorney does **not** authorize the agent to make health care decisions for you.

You should select someone you trust to serve as your agent. Unless you specify otherwise, generally the agent's authority will continue until you die or revoke the power of attorney or the agent resigns or is unable to act for you.

Your agent is entitled to reasonable compensation unless you state otherwise in the special instructions.

This form provides for designation of one agent. If you wish to name more than one agent you may name a co-agent in the special instructions. Co-agents are not required to act together unless you include that requirement in the special instructions. If your agent is unable or unwilling to act for you, your power of attorney will end unless you have named a successor agent. You may also name a second successor agent.

This power of attorney becomes effective immediately unless you state otherwise in the special instructions.

If you have questions about the power of attorney or the authority you are granting to your agent, you should seek legal advice before signing this form.

1. DESIGNATION OF AGENT

I _____ (name of principal) name the following person as my agent:
Name of agent: _____
Agent's address: _____
Agent's telephone number: _____

2. DESIGNATION OF SUCCESSOR AGENT(S) (OPTIONAL)

If my agent is unable or unwilling to act for me, I name as my successor agent:

Name of successor agent: _____
Successor agent's address: _____
Successor agent's telephone number: _____

If my successor agent is unable or unwilling to act for me, I name as second successor agent:
Name of second successor agent: _____
Second successor agent's address: _____
Second successor agent's telephone number: _____

3. GRANT OF GENERAL AUTHORITY

I grant my agent and any successor agent general authority to act for me with respect to the following subjects as defined in the "Uniform Power of Attorney Act", part 7 of article 14 of title 15, Colorado Revised Statutes:

(INITIAL each subject you want to include in the agent's general authority. If you wish to grant general authority over all of the subjects you may initial "All preceding subjects" instead of initialing each subject.)

(_____) A. Real property
(_____) B. Tangible personal property
(_____) C. Stocks and bonds
(_____) D. Commodities and options
(_____) E. Banks and other financial institutions
(_____) F. Operation of entity or business
(_____) G. Insurance and annuities
(_____) H. Estates, trusts, and other beneficial interests
(_____) I. Claims and litigation
(_____) J. Personal and family maintenance
(_____) K. Benefits from governmental programs or civil or military service
(_____) L. Retirement plans
(_____) M. Taxes
(_____) N. All preceding subjects

4. GRANT OF SPECIFIC AUTHORITY (OPTIONAL)

My agent MAY NOT do any of the following specific acts for me UNLESS I have INITIALED the specific authority listed below:

(CAUTION: Granting any of the following will give your agent the authority to take actions that could significantly reduce your property or change how your property is distributed at your death. INITIAL ONLY the specific authority you WANT to give your agent.)

(_____) A. Create, amend, revoke, or terminate an inter vivos trust
(_____) B. Make a gift, subject to the limitations of the "Uniform Power of Attorney Act" set forth in section 15-14-740, Colorado Revised Statutes, and any special instructions in this power of attorney
(_____) C. Create or change rights of survivorship
(_____) D. Create or change a beneficiary designation
(_____) E. Authorize another person to exercise authority granted under this power of attorney
(_____) F. Waive the principal's right to be a beneficiary of a joint and survivor annuity, including a survivor benefit under a retirement plan
(_____) G. Exercise fiduciary powers that the principal has authority to delegate, including powers to participate in the designation or changing of a fiduciary and powers to participate in the direction of a fiduciary in the exercise of the fiduciary's powers
(_____) H. Disclaim, refuse, or release an interest in property or a power of appointment

(____) I. Exercise a power of appointment other than: (1) The exercise of a general power of appointment for the benefit of the principal which may, if the subject of estates, trusts, and other beneficial interests is authorized above, be exercised as provided under the subject of estates, trusts, and other beneficial interests; or (2) the exercise of a general power of appointment for the benefit of persons other than the principal which may, if the making of a gift is specifically authorized above, be exercised under the specific authorization to make gifts

(____) J. Exercise powers, rights, or authority as a partner, member, or manager of a partnership, limited liability company, or other entity that the principal may exercise on behalf of the entity and has authority to delegate excluding the exercise of such powers, rights, and authority with respect to an entity owned solely by the principal which may, if operation of entity or business is authorized above, be exercised as provided under the subject of operation of the entity or business

5. LIMITATION ON AGENT'S AUTHORITY

An agent that is not my ancestor, spouse, or descendant MAY NOT use my property to benefit the agent or a person to whom the agent owes an obligation of support unless I have included that authority in the special instructions.

6. SPECIAL INSTRUCTIONS (OPTIONAL)

You may give special instructions on the following lines:

_____
_____
_____
_____
_____
_____

(long instructions are not recommended, but if needed attach additional pages)

7. EFFECTIVE DATE

This power of attorney is effective immediately unless I have stated otherwise in the special instructions.

8. NOMINATION OF CONSERVATOR OR GUARDIAN (OPTIONAL)

If it becomes necessary for a court to appoint a conservator of my estate or guardian of my person, I nominate the following person(s) for appointment:

Name of nominee for **conservator** of my estate: _____
Nominee's address: _____
Nominee's telephone number: _____

Name of nominee for **guardian** of my person: _____
Nominee's address: _____
Nominee's telephone number: _____

9. RELIANCE ON THIS POWER OF ATTORNEY

Any person, including my agent, may rely upon the validity of this power of attorney or a copy of it unless that person knows it has terminated or is invalid.

SIGNATURE AND ACKNOWLEDGMENT

_____ _____
Your signature   Date

_____ _____
Your name printed   Your telephone number

_____
Your address

WITNESS AFFIDAVIT (OPTIONAL)

We declare that, being first duly sworn, the principal signed and executed this instrument, knowingly and willingly, as the principal's Power of Attorney, and we signed this instrument as witnesses, in the conscious presence of the principal, and at the time of the execution of this instrument, the principal, according to our best knowledge and belief, was aware and of sound mind, and under no constraint or undue influence.

_____ _____
Witness #1 signature   Date

_____ _____
Witness #1 name printed   Witness #1 telephone number

_____ _____
Witness #2 signature   Date

_____ _____
Witness #2 name printed   Witness #2 telephone number

NOTARY

State of _____, County of _____) ss.

This document was acknowledged before me on _____, (Date) by _____ (Name of principal) and (if witnesses were used) subscribed and sworn to by _____ and _____ (Name of two witnesses).

Signature of notary: _____   (Seal, if any)
My commission expires: _____

Document prepared by (optional): _____

IMPORTANT INFORMATION FOR AGENT

Agent's duties

When you accept the authority granted under this power of attorney, a special legal relationship is created between you and the principal. This relationship imposes upon you legal duties that continue until you resign or the power of attorney is terminated or revoked. You must:

(1) Do what you know the principal reasonably expects you to do with the principal's property or, if you do not know the principal's expectations, act in the principal's best interest;
(2) Act in good faith;
(3) Do nothing beyond the authority granted in this power of attorney; and
(4) Disclose your identity as an agent whenever you act for the principal by writing or printing the name of the principal and signing your own name as "agent" in the following manner:
   (Principal's name) by (Your signature) as agent

Unless the special instructions in this power of attorney state otherwise, you must also:
(1) Act loyally for the principal's benefit;
(2) Avoid conflicts that would impair your ability to act in the principal's best interest;
(3) Act with care, competence, and diligence;
(4) Keep a record of all receipts, disbursements & transactions made on behalf of the principal;
(5) Cooperate with any person that has authority to make health care decisions for the principal to do what you know the principal reasonably expects or, if you do not know the principal's expectations, to act in the principal's best interest; and
(6) Attempt to preserve the principal's estate plan if you know the plan and preserving the plan is consistent with the principal's best interest.

Termination of agent's authority

You must stop acting on behalf of the principal if you learn of any event that terminates this power of attorney or your authority under this power of attorney. Events that terminate a power of attorney or your authority to act under a power of attorney include:
(1) Death of the principal;
(2) The principal's revocation of the power of attorney or your authority;
(3) The occurrence of a termination event stated in the power of attorney;
(4) The purpose of the power of attorney is fully accomplished; or
(5) If you are married to the principal, a legal action is filed with a court to end your marriage, or for your legal separation, unless the special instructions in this power of attorney state that such an action will not terminate your authority.

Liability of Agent

The meaning of the authority granted to you is defined in the "Uniform Power of Attorney Act", part 7 of article 14 of title 15, Colorado Revised Statutes. If you violate the "Uniform Power of Attorney Act", part 7 of article 14 of title 15, Colorado Revised Statutes, or act outside the authority granted, you may be liable for any damages caused by your violation.

IF THERE IS ANYTHING ABOUT THIS DOCUMENT OR YOUR DUTIES THAT YOU DO NOT UNDERSTAND, YOU SHOULD SEEK LEGAL ADVICE.

CHAPTER 16
FORM 10: POWER OF ATTORNEY BY PARENT OR GUARDIAN

FORM LETS A PARENT SHARE POWER WITH SOMEONE OVER A MINOR CHILD

This form lets a parent share power over a minor child under age 18 to someone to let them make decisions if needed. Note, besides a parent a guardian in charge of a child can also use this form.

FORM SHARES POWER OVER CHILD WITH SOMEONE

This form lets a parent share power over a minor child under age 18 with a person who is named in the form. In the form the parent is called the Principal and the person getting power is called the Agent or Attorney-in-Fact. The Agent can then make decisions about a child's school, healthcare, records, food, discipline, housing, travel, and more. Power is shared and the parent can usually over-rule or fire the Agent. Often named to be Agent is a family member, friend, teacher, or coach. The form gives no power over big issues like marriage, custody, or adoption. Doing this form may avoid need for more serious legal action like to temporary change in custody at court. Even if this form is not done usually doctors will provide emergency medical treatment to keep a child alive and avoid serious harm. This form is sometimes used if a parent and child are apart for work, school, prison, military, sports, immigration, and similar reasons. This form is usually not used for small events like a babysitter or few day visit with family or friends.

PEOPLE MUST SIGN FORM WITH A NOTARY

This form must be signed by a person in front of a person who is a notary who then notarizes the form. Once completed a person can keep the form until needed or hand it out immediately to the person named to be Agent in it. A few people quickly show the form to schools or doctors to get them to understand it should be followed later. The form can cover many children. The form often is slightly modified by people so both 2 parents can sign it to make the form seem more trustworthy and more likely to be followed.

POWER OF ATTORNEY BY PARENT OR GUARDIAN

(Pursuant to Colorado Revised Statutes § 15-14-105)

I, _____ (full name), parent or guardian of the minor child(ren) or incapacitated person(s) named below:

Full Name of Child or Incapacitated Person	Date of Birth	Relationship

I hereby authorize and appoint _____ (name of person), as Attorney in Fact for me with full authority to act in my place as follows:

1. To perform any and all acts necessary for the day-to-day care, custody, education, recreation, and property of the above-named minor child or incapacitated person, consistent with Colo. Rev. Stat. §15-14-105.

2. To authorize any and all medical and dental care for the health and well being of the minor child(ren) or incapacitated person(s). This care includes, but is not limited to medical and dental exams and tests, x-rays, surgeries, anesthesia, and hospital care.

This Special Power of Attorney does not give the Attorney in Fact the power to consent to the marriage or adoption of the child or incapacitated person.

This Special Power of Attorney shall be effective until _____ (date) unless revoked earlier by the parent or guardian in writing. In any case, the authority granted herein shall not be valid for more than 12 months from the date of this document.

Date: _____   _____
                                                    Parent/Guardian Signature

Subscribed and affirmed, or sworn to before me in _____ County, State of Colorado, this ____ day of _____, 20_____.

My Commission Expires: _____   _____
                                                                          Notary Public / Clerk

CHAPTER 17
FORM 11: DECLARATION OF DISPOSITION OF LAST REMAINS

FORM CAN COVER INSTRUCTIONS AND AGENT TO CONTROL BODILY REMAINS

This form lets a person give instructions about their body after death (their bodily remains) and also, if wanted, name someone as Agent to be in charge of this. This form is a statutory form found in state law.

FORM CAN NAME GIVE INSTRUCTIONS AND AGENT TO HANDLE DEAD BODY

This form lets a person (called the Declarant) give instructions and if wanted also pick someone (called the Designee) to control the person's dead body and related issues like funeral, burial, cremation, grave marker, ceremonies, and buying goods and services for this. <u>If this form is not done under state law control of all this is by closest family members</u> (in order this means a spouse, adult children, parents, and siblings). <u>People do this form rarely</u>, mostly only if it seems family would do a bad job like they may be too upset while mourning, be bad with money, or do unwanted things. Payment for burial, cremation, ceremonies, and related things will come from pre-paid funeral accounts, insurance, and a dead person's money and property, and the family and a person's Executor are legally required to help arrange payment if the estate can afford it. The form has an optional area to handle organ donation but this is usually better done in forms when doing a drivers license or state ID. People can skip any part of this form they want to.

FORM MUST BE SIGNED AND USING A WITNESS OR NOTARY IS COMMON

The form legally just must be signed and dated. Most people however also use 1 witness or a notary to make it more likely the form is followed. The completed form should be kept so it will be found within days of a death or it can given to a trusted person to hold. Most people verbally tell family what they want done. To cancel the form a person can tell people it is canceled or just make sure it is not found later after their death to be followed.

DECLARATION OF DISPOSITION OF LAST REMAINS
(Colorado Revised Statutes § 15-19-107)

I, _____ (name of Declarant), being of sound mind and lawful age, hereby revoke all prior declarations concerning the disposition of my last remains and those provisions concerning disposition of my last remains found in a will, codicil, or power of attorney, and I declare and direct that after my death the following provisions be taken:

1. If permitted by law, my body shall be (initial ONE choice):

_____ **Buried.** I direct that my body be buried at _____.

_____ **Cremated.** I direct that my cremated remains be disposed of as follows: _____
_____
_____.

_____ **Entombed.** I direct that my body be entombed at _____.

_____ **Naturally reduced.** I direct that my reduced remains be given final disposition as follows:
_____
_____.

_____ **Other.** I direct that my body be disposed of as follows:
_____
_____
_____.

_____ **Decision of my designee.** Disposed of as _____ (name of designee) shall decide in writing. If this person just named is unwilling or unable to act, I nominate _____ as my alternate designee.

2. I request the following ceremonial arrangements be made (initial desired choice or choices):

_____ **Decision of my designee.** I request _____ (name of designee) make all arrangements for any ceremonies, consistent with my directions set forth in this declaration. If this person just named is unwilling or unable to act, I nominate _____ as my alternate designee.

_____ **Funeral.** I request the following arrangements for my funeral:
_____
_____.

_____ **Memorial Service.** I request the following arrangements for my memorial service:
_____
_____.

3. Special instructions. In addition to the instructions above, I request (on the following lines you may make special requests regarding ceremonies or lack of ceremonies): _____
_____
_____.

I FULLY UNDERSTAND that I may revoke or amend this declaration in writing at any time. I agree that a third party who receives a copy of this declaration may act according to it. Revocation of this declaration is not effective as to a third party until the third party learns of my revocation. My estate shall indemnify any third party for costs incurred as a result of claims that arise against the third party because of good-faith reliance on this declaration.

I execute this declaration as my free and voluntary act, on _____, 20____.

        Declarant signature:_____

THE FOLLOWING SECTION REGARDING ORGAN AND TISSUE DONATION IS ALL OPTIONAL. To make a donation, initial the option you select and sign below.

In the hope that I might help others, I hereby make an anatomical gift, to be effective upon my death, of:

A._____ Any needed organs/tissues

B._____ The following organs/tissues: _____
_____.

        Donor signature:_____

NOTARIZATION (OR WITNESS) OPTIONAL:

Witness:

I am a competent witness at least age 18 who was present when declarant signed this declaration.

        Witness signature:_____

Notary:

STATE OF COLORADO   )
) ss.
COUNTY OF _____)

Acknowledged before me by _____, Declarant, on _____, 20___.

[seal]   Notary Public signature:_____
                                                   My commission expires:_____

APPENDIX :
HOW TO GET FORMS AND SAMPLE FILLED OUT FORMS

TO GET FORMS TO USE PEOPLE CAN:
   (1) PHOTOCOPY BOOK PAGES,
   (2) CUT AND TEAR OUT PAGES FROM THE PAPER BOOK, OR
   (3) DOWNLOAD BOOK WITH FORMS FROM <u>WWW.DAVENPORTPUBLISHING.COM</u>
AND <u>USUALLY PDF FORM AT IS BEST</u> TO AVOID SPACING/FORMAT CHANGES.

EMAIL ANY COMMENTS TO <u>DAVENPORTPRESS@GMAIL.COM</u> .

On the next pages to show how it can be done are some sample filled out legal forms.

People can add words to legal forms by computer or typewriter to be neater, but many people just by hand use pen, marker, or pencil to handwrite words into forms.

It is not required but is bit better if signatures are in ink or marker not pencil.

Many parts of the forms especially Will gifts can be left empty and unfilled.

Anyone can fill in words in legal form not just the person doing the form, like a friend with neat writing can fill in all the words, addresses, and dates that are needed. <u>Only the final signatures must be done by each person who wants the</u> form.

To add words in form by pen, pencil, typewriter, or computer any of these is fine:
        "I appoint _*John Doe*_ as Agent",
        "I appoint __John Doe__ as Agent",
        "I appoint John Doe as Agent".

When doing forms it may help to know "respectively" means "in order just stated".

People need not worry about neatness or small mistakes, and a document is usually fine if those people who knew a decedent in life can tell the likely meaning.

Sample Filled Out Form: Last Will and Testament (Standard) with Gifts section skipped to not bother making small gifts

LAST WILL AND TESTAMENT

I am _Paul Samuel Maxwell_ of _Larimer County_, Colorado and I revoke all prior Wills and testamentary documents and do make, publish, and declare this as my Will. I am of sound mind and under no duress or undue influence and acting voluntarily.

1. LIST OF SPOUSE AND CHILDREN. To help show I am mentally competent and have sufficient memory to make a Will I wish to list any living spouse and living children I now have. I currently have the following living spouse and living children:

none

2. GIFTS. I give these gifts in this Will, but to get a gift in this section the recipient must survive me except as otherwise stated below.

I give _____ to _____.
I give _____ to _____.
I give _____ to _____.
I give _____ to _____.
I give _____ to _____.
I give _____ to _____.

3. SEPARATE WRITINGS. I may do writings separate from this Will to gift tangible personal property as allowed by state law, and all such writings should be followed. But any such writing not found within 90 days of my death is canceled and has no effect. A gift in such a writing to a person who does not survive me is canceled and has no effect. This Will does not revoke any such writings that now exist.

4. RESIDUE. I give the rest and residue and remainder of my estate, my money and property of any kind and nature, and anything I have an interest in so long as it was not transferred by other Will provisions (all of which is called the "residue"), as follows:

   a) to _Susan Lee Maxwell my sister_ who survive me with persons just named who survive me taking the share of non-survivors, then if anything remains

   b) to _Oscar David Maxwell and Jennifer Judy Tabor_ and if any of those just named do not survive me their part goes to their lineal descendants, per stirpes.

5. ADMINISTRATION. I nominate and appoint _Susan Lee Maxwell_
as Personal Representative including for me, my Will, and my estate.

6. MISCELLANEOUS. The following applies to this Will and generally.

In this Will no part left unfilled is a mistake including spaces in the residue clause.

The facts support and I want Colorado state law to apply to this Will and my estate.

I order that my just debts, funeral and related expenses, and taxes be paid as soon after my death as practical but only those items my Personal Representative chooses to pay.

Priority of Will gifts of the same type is based on the order they are written.

The words "give" and "gift" also means a devise, bequest, grant, legacy, or similar.

I am intentionally not providing by Will or other ways for some family, including I am not providing for some children of mine and also children of a deceased child of mine.

If a gift Will reasonably mentions survival then survival is an absolute condition and anti-lapse laws or similar provisions have no effect and without survival the gift lapses. Unless a Will gift specifies otherwise if a Will gift goes to multiple recipients if any do not survive me the part to them lapses and instead goes to other surviving recipients.

No earlier transfer reduces a Will gift unless I usually called it a loan or advancement.

Unless another meaning is shown use of plural includes the singular and vice versa, and "they" can mean 1 person. Masculine, feminine, and neuter words are interchangeable.

Unless a Will specifically says otherwise a secured debt including a mortgage or lien shall not be paid off including by a Personal Representative or in probate, and a recipient of a Will gift of property takes it subject to debts. Also, no recipient of property who may lose it or who pays to keep it may have my estate or others pay or do exoneration.

If during my life I disposed of an item in a specific gift then the gift is extinguished.

I request and authorize any informal, summary, and quick probate or similar action. Any Personal Representative may act independently with no supervision of any court, including independent administration, and with no inventory, appraisal, or other action.

I give any Personal Representative the a) fullest authority, discretion, and powers allowed by state law, b) power to lease, sell, mortgage, convey, or keep property including real property in a manner and time they deem helpful or proper, and c) authority to settle or pay claims or debts in the time and manner they in their sole discretion choose.

A Personal Representative may request and be paid reasonable compensation.

Any Guardian of any type, Conservator, Custodian, or other person managing a minor's property or money may use or invade the principal and sell property without court action.

If context permits the terms Personal Representative and Executor and Administrator are interchangeable, Guardian of Property and Conservator and Guardian of the Estate and Custodian are interchangeable, and residue and residuary are interchangeable. Any such person may stand in the place of and have all powers like the others named here.

The residue includes lapsed or failed gifts, insurance paid to the estate, digital assets, inheritances owed me, and all I had power of appointment or testamentary disposition over.

Any Personal Representative, Executor, Administrator, Guardian of any type like for a person or estate, Conservator, Custodian, and any other fiduciary under this Will or otherwise shall qualify and serve without bond, surety, security, surety bond, or similar.

If evidence does not show it likely a person survived me by 120 hours (5 days) then for this Will and my estate they shall be deemed in all ways as having died before me.

If part of this Will is by law invalid or unenforceable other provisions remain in effect.

Any Personal Representative may at any time transfer money or property of a minor under age 18 to a Custodian to serve under the Colorado Uniform Transfers to Minors Act or a similar law anywhere, and may pick the person to be Custodian including themselves.

TESTATOR

IN WITNESS WHEREOF, I, _Paul Samuel Maxwell_, the Testator, declare that this instrument is my Will which I make as Testator, that I do this as a free and voluntary act for the purposes expressed therein, that I am at least 18 years of age and of sound mind and under no constraint or undue influence, and that I do sign this instrument voluntarily as my Will in the presence and sight of each of the two witnesses who are named and who sign below, this _8th_ day of _June_, 20_22_.

Paul Samuel Maxwell
Testator signature

WITNESSES

We, _Eve Mable Walker_ and _Susan Ann Moon_, the Witnesses, sign our names to this instrument, and do hereby declare to everyone (including any undersigned authority to which we may have been sworn) that the Testator signs and executes this instrument as the Will of the Testator and that the Testator signs it willingly, and that the Testator executes it as the Testator's free and voluntary act for the purposes therein expressed, and that each of us, in the conscious presence of the Testator, hereby at Testator's request signs this Will to witness the Testator's signing, and that to the best of our knowledge the Testator is 18 years of age or older, of sound mind, and under no constraint or undue influence.

Eve Mable Walker   _35 Buffalo Road, Denver, Colorado 80101_
Witness #1 signature   Witness #1 address

Susan Ann Moon   _14 2nd St., Miami, FL 34787_
Witness #2 signature   Witness #2 address

**Sample Filled Out Form: Last Will and Testament (Guardian)
with many gifts in Gifts section, Guardian Clause used, and Residue Given By Percentages**

LAST WILL AND TESTAMENT

I am Paul Brian Baker of Boulder County , Colorado and I revoke all prior Wills and testamentary documents and do make, publish, and declare this as my Will. I am of sound mind and under no duress or undue influence and acting voluntarily.

1. LIST OF SPOUSE AND CHILDREN. To help show I am mentally competent and have sufficient memory to make a Will I wish to list any living spouse and living children I now have. I currently have the following living spouse and living children:

_____Ruth May Baker wife_____ _____Oscar Elliot Baker young son_____
_____Karen Lisa Lundy daughter_____ Derek Rupert Baker son _____.

2. GIFTS. I give these gifts in this Will, but to get a gift in this section the recipient must survive me except as otherwise stated below.

I give _____big oak table_____ to _____Anne J. Smith_____.

I give $5,000 and Ford Truck to Loretta Marsha Baxter .

I give buildings, land, and fixtures at 63 Wentworth Road, Denver, Colorado
to Kenneth Alan Ford .

I give all real property and fixtures I own in Boulder County in Colorado to Amy Marie Fox and Pamela Sue Fox .

I give 903 Iceberg Road, Anchorage, Alaska to James Eric Hanson .

I give Irish jewelry and my wedding ring to Mary Natalie Swanson .

I give all jewelry not given above to Kay Baxter and Mary Baxter .

I give $781.35 to Mary Natalie Swanson and Kevin Kilby .

I give Wells Fargo acct ending in #8923 to Lawrence Deer a hunting buddy .

I give all spare tires and auto parts to Victor Perez my mechanic .

I give _____ to _____.

3. SEPARATE WRITINGS. I may do writings separate from this Will to gift tangible personal property as allowed by state law, and all such writings should be followed. But any such writing not found within 90 days of my death is canceled and has no effect. A gift in such a writing to a person who does not survive me is canceled and has no effect. This Will does not revoke any such writings that now exist.

4. RESIDUE. I give the rest and residue and remainder of my estate, my money and property of any kind and nature, and anything I have an interest in so long as it was not transferred by other Will provisions (all of which is called the "residue"), as follows:

  a) to _____Ruth May Baker_____ who survive me with persons just named who survive me taking the share of non-survivors, then if anything remains

  b) to __45% to Oscar Elliot Baker, and 45% to Karen Lisa Lundy, and 10% to Luis Sanchez my friend_____ and if any of those just named do not survive me their part goes to their lineal descendants, per stirpes.

5. ADMINISTRATION. I nominate and appoint __Ruth May Baker_____ as Personal Representative including for me, my Will, and my estate.

6. GUARDIAN. I name, nominate, and appoint _Amanda Sue Brubaker my sister_ to be Guardian of any minor child of mine and also to have care, authority, custody, and other control of them (including as Guardian of the Person). I also name this same person to be Conservator for any minor child of mine and also to have care, control, and power over their property, money, and estate (including as Guardian of the Estate).

7. MISCELLANEOUS. The following applies to this Will and generally.

  In this Will no part left unfilled is a mistake including spaces in the residue clause.

  The facts support and I want Colorado state law to apply to this Will and my estate.

  I order that my just debts, funeral and related expenses, and taxes be paid as soon after my death as practical but only those items my Personal Representative chooses to pay.

  Priority of Will gifts of the same type is based on the order they are written.

  The words "give" and "gift" also means a devise, bequest, grant, legacy, or similar.

  I am intentionally not providing by Will or other ways for some family, including I am not providing for some children of mine and also children of a deceased child of mine.

  If a gift Will reasonably mentions survival then survival is an absolute condition and anti-lapse laws or similar provisions have no effect and without survival the gift lapses. Unless a Will gift specifies otherwise if a Will gift goes to multiple recipients if any do not survive me the part to them lapses and instead goes to other surviving recipients.

  No earlier transfer reduces a Will gift unless I usually called it a loan or advancement.

  Unless another meaning is shown use of plural includes the singular and vice versa, and "they" can mean 1 person. Masculine, feminine, and neuter words are interchangeable.

  If during my life I disposed of an item in a specific gift then the gift is extinguished.

  I give any Personal Representative the a) fullest authority, discretion, and powers allowed by state law, b) power to lease, sell, mortgage, convey, or keep property including real property in a manner and time they deem helpful or proper, and c) authority to settle or pay claims or debts in the time and manner they in their sole discretion choose.

  A Personal Representative may request and be paid reasonable compensation.

  Any Guardian of any type, Conservator, Custodian, or other person managing a minor's

property or money may use or invade the principal and sell property without court action.

The residue includes lapsed or failed gifts, insurance paid to the estate, digital assets, inheritances owed me, and all I had power of appointment or testamentary disposition over.

Any Personal Representative, Executor, Administrator, Guardian of any type like for a person or estate, Conservator, Custodian, and any other fiduciary under this Will or otherwise shall qualify and serve without bond, surety, security, surety bond, or similar.

If evidence does not show it likely a person survived me by 120 hours (5 days) then for this Will and my estate they shall be deemed in all ways as having died before me.

If part of this Will is by law invalid or unenforceable other provisions remain in effect.

Any Personal Representative may at any time transfer money or property of a minor under age 18 to a Custodian to serve under the Colorado Uniform Transfers to Minors Act or a similar law anywhere, and may pick the person to be Custodian including themselves.

TESTATOR

IN WITNESS WHEREOF, I, _Paul Brian Baker_, the Testator, declare that this instrument is my Will which I make as Testator, that I do this as a free and voluntary act for the purposes expressed therein, that I am at least 18 years of age and of sound mind and under no constraint or undue influence, and that I do sign this instrument voluntarily as my Will in the presence and sight of each of the two witnesses who are named and who sign below, this _30th_ day of _December_, 20_21_.

Paul Brian Baker
Testator signature

WITNESSES

We, _Olivia Anna Paulson_ and _Matthew John Paulson_, the Witnesses, sign our names to this instrument, and do hereby declare to everyone (including any undersigned authority to which we may have been sworn) that the Testator signs and executes this instrument as the Will of the Testator and that the Testator signs it willingly, and that the Testator executes it as the Testator's free and voluntary act for the purposes therein expressed, and that each of us, in the conscious presence of the Testator, hereby at Testator's request signs this Will to witness the Testator's signing, and that to the best of our knowledge the Testator is 18 years of age or older, of sound mind, and under no constraint or undue influence.

Olivia Anna Paulson _82 Forest Road, Lakewood, CO 80134_
Witness #1 signature   Witness #1 address

Matthew John Paulson _82 Forest Road, Lakewood, CO 80134_
Witness #2 signature   Witness #2 address

**Sample Filled Out Form: Last Will and Testament (Standard)
with Will modified to have a 1 Part Residue Clause**

LAST WILL AND TESTAMENT

I, __John David Smith__ of __Arapahoe County__, Colorado and I revoke all prior Wills and testamentary documents and do make, publish, and declare this as my Will. I am of sound mind and under no duress or undue influence and acting voluntarily.

1. LIST OF SPOUSE AND CHILDREN. To help show I am mentally competent and have sufficient memory to make a Will I wish to list any living spouse and living children I now have. I currently have the following living spouse and living children:

___my son Adam Michael Smith___

_____.

2. GIFTS. I give these gifts in this Will, but to get a gift in this section the recipient must survive me except as otherwise stated below.

I give __$200__ to __each of my nieces and nephews so about $2,800 in total__.

I give __$400__ to __Garner Food Shelf in Fort Collins, Colorado__.

I give __$340__ to __Sunset Park Christian Church in Pueblo, Colorado__.

I give _____ to _____.

I give _____ to _____.

I give _____ to _____.

I give _____ to _____.

I give _____ to _____.

I give _____ to _____.

I give _____ to _____.

3. SEPARATE WRITINGS. I may do writings separate from this Will to gift tangible personal property as allowed by state law, and all such writings should be followed. But any such writing not found within 90 days of my death is canceled and has no effect. A gift in such a writing to a person who does not survive me is canceled and has no effect. This Will does not revoke any such writings that now exist.

4. RESIDUE. The rest and residue and remainder of my estate, my property of any kind and nature, and anything I have an interest in, I give to <u>　Adam Michael Smith and Judy Paula Ford　</u> who survive me and to the lineal descendants per stirpes of a person just named who did not survive me.

5. ADMINISTRATION. I nominate and appoint <u>　Judy Paula Ford my sister　</u> as Personal Representative including for me, my Will, and my estate.

6. MISCELLANEOUS. The following applies to this Will and generally.

In this Will no part left unfilled is a mistake including spaces in the residue clause.

The facts support and I want Colorado state law to apply to this Will and my estate.

I order that my just debts, funeral and related expenses, and taxes be paid as soon after my death as practical but only those items my Personal Representative chooses to pay.

Priority of Will gifts of the same type is based on the order they are written.

The words "give" and "gift" also means a devise, bequest, grant, legacy, or similar.

I am intentionally not providing by Will or other ways for some family, including I am not providing for some children of mine and also children of a deceased child of mine.

If a gift Will reasonably mentions survival then survival is an absolute condition and anti-lapse laws or similar provisions have no effect and without survival the gift lapses. Unless a Will gift specifies otherwise if a Will gift goes to multiple recipients if any do not survive me the part to them lapses and instead goes to other surviving recipients.

No earlier transfer reduces a Will gift unless I usually called it a loan or advancement.

Unless another meaning is shown use of plural includes the singular and vice versa, and "they" can mean 1 person. Masculine, feminine, and neuter words are interchangeable.

Unless a Will specifically says otherwise a secured debt including a mortgage or lien shall not be paid off including by a Personal Representative or in probate, and a recipient of a Will gift of property takes it subject to debts. Also, no recipient of property who may lose it or who pays to keep it may have my estate or others pay or do exoneration.

If during my life I disposed of an item in a specific gift then the gift is extinguished.

I request and authorize any informal, summary, and quick probate or similar action. Any Personal Representative may act independently with no supervision of any court, including independent administration, and with no inventory, appraisal, or other action.

I give any Personal Representative the a) fullest authority, discretion, and powers allowed by state law, b) power to lease, sell, mortgage, convey, or keep property including real property in a manner and time they deem helpful or proper, and c) authority to settle or pay claims or debts in the time and manner they in their sole discretion choose.

A Personal Representative may request and be paid reasonable compensation.

Any Guardian of any type, Conservator, Custodian, or other person managing a minor's property or money may use or invade the principal and sell property without court action.

If context permits the terms Personal Representative and Executor and Administrator are interchangeable, Guardian of Property and Conservator and Guardian of the Estate and

Custodian are interchangeable, and residue and residuary are interchangeable. Any such person may stand in the place of and have all powers like the others named here.

The residue includes lapsed or failed gifts, insurance paid to the estate, digital assets, inheritances owed me, and all I had power of appointment or testamentary disposition over.

Any Personal Representative, Executor, Administrator, Guardian of any type like for a person or estate, Conservator, Custodian, and any other fiduciary under this Will or otherwise shall qualify and serve without bond, surety, security, surety bond, or similar.

If evidence does not show it likely a person survived me by 120 hours (5 days) then for this Will and my estate they shall be deemed in all ways as having died before me.

If part of this Will is by law invalid or unenforceable other provisions remain in effect.

Any Personal Representative may at any time transfer money or property of a minor under age 18 to a Custodian to serve under the Colorado Uniform Transfers to Minors Act or a similar law anywhere, and may pick the person to be Custodian including themselves.

TESTATOR

IN WITNESS WHEREOF, I, ___John David Smith___, the Testator, declare, sign, and publish this instrument as my Will, this _21st_ day of ___June___, 20_23_.

John David Smith
Testator Signature

WITNESSES

The foregoing instrument was signed by the Testator and Testator declared it to be the Testator's Will, which signing and declaration was made in the presence of us the Witnesses, and we do now sign our names in this document below acting as witnesses at the request and in the presence of the Testator and presence of each other on this _21st_ day of ___June___, 20_23_.

Mark Elliot Potter
Witness Signature
___Mark Elliot Potter, 2 Spruce St, Sherwood, CO 80411___
Printed Name and Residence of Witness

Ann Paula Blom
Witness Signature
___Ann Paula Blom, 70 Rocky Road, Clarksville, Colorado 80124___
Printed Name and Residence of Witness

Sample Filled Out Form: Self-Proving Affidavit

SELF-PROVING AFFIDAVIT

(Colorado Revised Statutes § 15-11-504 (2))

THE STATE OF COLORADO

COUNTY OF ____ARAPAHOE____

We, __John David Smith__, __Mark Elliot Potter__, and __Ann Paula Blom__, the Testator and the Witnesses, respectively, whose names are signed to the attached or foregoing instrument, being first duly sworn, do hereby declare to the undersigned authority that the Testator signed and executed the instrument as the Testator's Will and that the Testator had signed willingly (or willingly directed another to sign for the Testator), and that the Testator executed it as Testator's free and voluntary act for the purposes therein expressed, and that each of the Witnesses, in the conscious presence of the Testator, signed the Will acting as a witness and that to the best of the knowledge of all Witnesses the Testator was at that time 18 years of age or older, of sound mind, and under no constraint or undue influence.

_____*John David Smith*_____
Testator

__*Mark Elliot Potter*__ __*Ann Paula Blom*__
Witness Witness

Subscribed, sworn to, and acknowledged before me by __John David Smith__, the Testator, and subscribed and sworn to before me by __Mark Elliot Potter__ and __Anna Paula Blom__, Witnesses, this __21st__ day of __June__, 20__23__.

(SEAL, if any)

NICOLAS WILLIAMS
NOTARY PUBLIC STATE OF COLORADO
NOTARY ID 981537439
MY COMMISSION EXPIRES FEB 9, 2029

(SIGNED) __*Nicholas Williams*__
(Official capacity of officer) _____

Sample Filled Out Form: Tangible Personal Property List

TANGIBLE PERSONAL PROPERTY LIST

In this writing are gifts of tangible personal property to occur at my death, but this writing if not found by someone within 90 days of my death is canceled.

I may do many pages of these writings which should all be seen as one document. If there are conflicts among such writings the provisions of the more recent writing will revoke the inconsistent provisions of a prior writing.

If a person getting a gift below does not survive me such gift is void and canceled.

DESCRIPTION OF PROPERTY	NAMES OF RECIPIENTS
1998 Ford Truck	Samantha Bell
1.3 carat diamond ring + Irish rings	Ann Sue Reed
14 ft power boat + kayak + paddles	L. Wheeler
Amish style bench	Reba Stewart
glass table, telescope, umbrellas	Rebecca Stewart
Irish wood cups, oak platter, red vase	Mary and Cindy Lott
painting of sailboat in storm	Mary Lott
chainsaw with number 382937	Mary Lott
chainsaw with number 89930	Matt Smith
antique lanterns + repair kits	Sue Wu maid at Hart Hotel
lamp kept on porch	Mary Kay Poppler
sewing machines	Mary Kay Poppler
rocking chair bought in Oregon	Don Winkler boat mechanic
all fishing poles and fishing nets	Joe "Fish" Hoss, fishing pal
hats at cabin	Ken Baker
all clothing except hats at cabin	Melissa and Wendy Smith

DATE: 5-15-2024   SIGNED: John David Smith